PRINCE CHARLES

PRINCE CHARLES

The Biography

by

HELEN CATHCART

TAPLINGER PUBLISHING COMPANY
NEW YORK

First published in the United States in 1977 by
TAPLINGER PUBLISHING CO., INC.
New York, New York

Library of Congress Catalog Card Number: 77-73686

ISBN 0-8008-6555-3

Contents

Illustrations

Author's Note

It is nearly ten years since Dermot Morrah wrote his definitive study of the boyhood and education of H.R.H. The Prince of Wales, *To Be a King*. I have felt similarly privileged in giving this account of the life – and life style – of Prince Charles to the present day, not least as he nears the intended conclusion of his naval career and approaches the happy turning-point he has described as 'one of the most responsible steps to be taken in one's life'.

The literature on the Heir Apparent is already considerable, but I have attempted a fresh portrait of 'the Prince in person', drawn from sources as wide and diverse as possible. Much private material has been released to benefit my narrative and I am more than grateful to those who took pains to clarify the necessary detail. Throughout my consultations I received direct information on every point requested, as well as kindly guidance against the risks of error.

In acknowledgement of published sources, a bibliography is appended, and I have to add that the copyright in quotations from royal correspondence, journals and associated material is reserved.

HELEN CATHCART

1 A Prince of Edinburgh

I

Within the warm domestic circle of the House and Family of Windsor in 1948, some thirty years after King George V first proclaimed the new-chosen name of his dynasty, Prince Charles was the first-born of a happy and highly popular young couple. The Queen, then Princess Elizabeth, was just twenty-two when her pregnancy was made known, while Prince Philip, Duke of Edinburgh, was twenty-six, still foremost a naval officer by profession, though gaining a sense of deeper vocation after six months of marriage to the heiress-presumptive to the throne.

Behind these two reach qualities of heredity that have already caused the personality of Prince Charles to be more assiduously studied and underscored by historians than that of any other young man of our contemporary world. He is thirty-second in descent, direct as may be, from William the Conqueror, and thirty-ninth from Alfred the Great, through the line that some scholars trace back beyond Egbert, the first King of All England, and farther back for another three hundred years of the successive Kings of Wessex. He is also twenty-third in descent from Robert the Bruce through Mary, Queen of Scots, or a generation closer via the Bowes-Lyons. He rightly wears the Royal Stuart tartan as thirteenth in line from Charles I, and through that monarch's eldest daughter he descends from the Electress Sophia whose title under the Act of Settlement firmly roots his succession to the Crown.

On his father's side, Prince Charles comes of an even more powerful line of Scandinavian counts and dukes and kings, claiming family records link upon link through five centuries

There are other lines for those who care to browse through such forebears: the Dukes of Normandy and the House of Anjou, or back by way of the Anglo-Danish kings to Canute, grandson of Harald Blue-tooth, King of Denmark.

'I suppose I am a mixture of all my ancestors in one,' says Charles. On his mother's side alone the compound is bewilderingly English, Scottish, Welsh, Danish, Germanic, Dutch, French and Russian, with traces of Spanish, Portuguese and other elements sufficient for the Common Market community to view him as a characteristic contemporary synthesis of European man.

As Prince of Wales, the twenty-first English successor in that title, he also descends – through Henry Tudor – from Llewellyn-ap-Gruffyd, the last native Prince of All Wales.

Prince Charles takes a lively interest in such patterns and, when he has the leisure, delves with relish into the lives and experience of his forefathers. The historian, John Brooke, while researching the life and personality of George III in the archives at Windsor, met the Prince enthusiastically engaged in the same occupation and, according to the Prince, they 'had a long and intriguing conversation'. Original sources can correct subsequent misconceptions. 'As human beings,' Charles wrote later, 'we suffer from an innate tendency to jump to conclusions; to judge people too quickly and to pronounce them failures or heroes without due consideration.'

At the same time, Charles takes a droll delight in some of the more goonish characters hidden within the foliage of his family tree: Sweyn Forkbeard and his son-in-law, Ulf Sprakalegg; Wig, the son of Freawine, the son of Frithugar, the son of Brand, the son of Baeldaeg and similar characters surely derived from an ad lib Saxon patter book. The obligatory cattle thief and pirate appears in Rollo the Ganger, whose island lair our present Queen was once invited to include in her itinerary of a visit to Norway, the ganger – or gangster – who ravaged northern France in the year 876 and gained the dukedom of Normandy from a monarch curtly known as Charles the Simple. There is also the shade of

William Longsword, his sword of insufficient length to prevent his own murder, and the merry ghost of King Cole or Ceol who reigned in Wessex for a genial four years.

Among the unlikely ladies we find Melesende, Queen of Jerusalem, the second wife of one of Prince Charles' Plantagenet forebears, and then there is the far-roaming Gytha, elder daughter of the King Harold who fell at Hastings in 1066, from whom in turn Prince Charles is reckoned thirty-second in descent. After various wanderings, Gytha married the improbably named Vladimir Monomakh, Great Prince of Kiev, and it may be true that, when Princess Anne defended her European riding title at Kiev, Prince Charles lightly enjoined his sister to pay her respects to 'great-great-many times – grandmama', for Gytha is buried there.

Then, in more modern times there has emerged a link of cousinhood with George Washington eight times removed, not to mention kinship with Robert E. Lee and a link through Charles' maternal great-great-grandfather, the 13th Earl of Strathmore, with a cousin who fathered the little girl forever remembered as Alice in Wonderland.

In the wonderland of the genes the Prince of Wales is also, through his maternal grandmother and all his Bowes-Lyon kith and kin, the most Scottish prince since Charles I and perhaps the most English of princes since Henry VIII. Charles may claim to be the most democratic Prince of Wales ever bred. In the Queen Mother's ancestry, only four generations removed, are Smiths and Tuckers, honest builders and farmers, and great-great-grandmamas of plain name such as Mary Carpenter and Charlotte Walsh, Frances Webb and Mary Browne.

In contrast, Prince Philip's lesser-known and yet enlivening ancestry includes in the eighteenth century the handsome figure of the Duke Peter August, an Imperial Russian Field Marshal, who, being a widower at thirty-one, served Catherine the Great and served her so well that he swiftly rose to be Governor-General of Estonia. And in the middle of the last century there occurs the beautiful and romantically orphaned Julie Hauke, who ran away with Prince Alexander of Hesse in a midnight elopement and, all being eventually forgiven, became a Princess of Battenberg and Prince Philip's maternal great-grandmother.

Through both Philip and the Queen, Prince Charles of course stems fifth in descent from Queen Victoria. Yet in these strange days of ours it has also been properly pointed out, in a 1971–72 report from the Select Committee on Race Relations, that since one of his parents was born outside the British Isles – and Prince Philip was undeniably born in Corfu – the Prince of Wales can by definition be classified as an immigrant.

II

'She was frightfully pleased,' one of the Queen's earliest intimates has chattily recorded of the days when Elizabeth awaited her first baby. 'It was what she wanted most.' From a storeroom in Royal Lodge, her parents' Windsor retreat, she looked out the old high-slung pram used in turn by both herself and Princess Margaret in babyhood, and when it had been refurbished and had arrived safely at Buckingham Palace, she wheeled it along the corridor, thoughtfully judging the wheels and balance and springing. 'Look,' she announced, bright as the pram itself, 'I'm getting my hand in.'

The old cast-iron cot was found, and trimmed with yellow silk by two elderly needlewomen in South London. An old basket appeared, silk-covered and lace-trimmed to match. These were the days, three years after the 1939-45 war, when every nursery necessity was in short supply, so much so that Prince Philip hilariously looked out his own baby clothes one afternoon in case they might serve. 'It gave him a sense of roots, of belonging,' his cousin, Queen Alexandra of Yugoslavia, defined his happy, paternal mood. 'Philip never had much of his own,' and she recollected the nursery tale that in their infancy in Athens they had often shared prams.

In 1948, indeed, Elizabeth and Philip still had no real home of their own. Earlier in the year they had borrowed the Clock House at Kensington Palace from the Athlones for a few months and obviously revelled in their romantic privacy on the staff night off. Clarence House was still in the throes of being made ready for them, and that summer they rented Windlesham Moor, the lush former home of a City financier, more as a convenient stopgap than for any admiration of its green marble columns and vast mirrored closets, its fifty-foot drawing-room and spacious nursery and bedroom suites. But when the question of where her baby should be born arose for discussion, Princess Elizabeth insisted that she wanted it to be at home, meaning Buckingham Palace, 'in my own room, amongst the things I know'.

In any event, surgery had to be prepared at the Palace that autumn for the medical needs of King George VI, whose doctors were becoming increasingly concerned about his state of health. The choice fell on the Buhl Room on the first floor, in the suite adjoining the Centre Room with its famous balcony. The old-fashioned inlaid ebony and tortoise-shell furnishings were moved out to make way for modern clinical equipment, and on November 12th the King underwent a minor operation to relieve an arterial obstruction of the right leg. This marked the first of the three operations in the final tragic years of his life, and his grandson, a presumptive future King, was to be born in the same room two days later. The Buhl Room had been little used since the King's Coronation, but within the passage of sixty hours it was thus the background of two dynastic events of great consequence.

With her sense of physical well-being and her imaginative orchestration of events, the Princess had thought that her baby might not arrive until November 20th, the first anniversary of her wedding. On the evening of November 12th she drove with her husband to dine with her friends and cousins-in-law, Lord and Lady Brabourne, at 16 Chester Street, reassured on her father's progress and equally convinced that her midwife, Miss Rowe, was fussing too soon.

On Sunday November 14th, however, the crowds gathered outside Buckingham Palace, drawn mysteriously as crowds have always been by the magnetism of royal events. No mere cluster of casual tourists and sightseers, but the largest assembly since Princess Elizabeth's wedding-day presently extended from the sentry walk outside the gilt-tipped Palace railings across the road to the Victoria Memorial. There was little to see, except the martial disciplines of the changing of the guardsmen and the coming and going of cars containing inscrutable gentlemen, but still the crowd accumulated, steadfast and waiting.

An incautious newspaper had announced some months earlier that 'the King and Queen and other members of the royal family' were 'to register for free medical attention under the new National Health Service', but it is doubtful whether this applied to Sir John Weir, the King's physician, Mr John Peel, the gynaecologist, or Dr Vernon Hall, the anaesthetist from King's College Hospital, who had slipped into Buckingham Palace earlier that day. When the forecourt lamps came on in the November dusk, the police at last gave up their cries of 'keep the roadway clear, please!', and people shouted 'We want Philip!', as if absurdly expecting him to appear upon the balcony.

One Palace onlooker estimated the crowd at three or four thousand, 'making little noise', but presently the waiting throng began singing *Rule, Britannia*, *For He's a Jolly Good Fellow*, snatches from *Oklahoma* and, prophetically, from a Welsh contingent, *Land of our Fathers*. Then, in the darkness, *Happy Birthday to You* was taken up vociferously, and some muted welcoming murmur of that song must have drifted through the closed curtains of the Buhl Room.

As is well known, Prince Philip passed the waiting hours playing sessions of squash on the Palace court with his private secretary and old naval friend, Lieutenant-Commander Michael Parker.

An absentee from the protocol of a royal birth was the Home Secretary, Mr Chuter Ede. The King had enquired some months earlier into the constitutional necessity of his traditional presence, and found it 'a practice for which there is no legal requirement'.

Shortly after nine fifteen p.m. the King's secretary, Sir Alan Lascelles, took the news to Prince Philip, 'It's a boy!' and the jubilant father raced up the stairs, three at a time, to the King and Queen in their sitting-room. The first outward telephone call from the Palace was made to the Home Secretary, but the first written message, rushed through the streets by an army dispatch rider, was addressed to the Lord Mayor of London in accordance with ancient privilege. Meanwhile, the King's press secretary, Commander Richard Colville, wrote out the first bulletin in his firm hand and took pride in ceremoniously carrying it across the Palace forecourt to see it affixed to the railings:

> *November 14th, 1948*
> *The Princess Elizabeth, Duchess of Edinburgh, was safely delivered of a Prince at 9.14 p.m. Her Royal Highness and her son are both doing well.*

The roar of cheering at the sight of the framed announcement was heard deep inside the Palace and can still be heard on a BBC recording. Then the songs were resumed, *Happy Birthday* and *For He's a Jolly Good Fellow*, again and again. From the direction of the Mall, towards eleven p.m., a swelling burst of cheers and applause heralded the arrival of the baby's first outside visitor, the indefatigable Queen Mary, then in her eighty-second year, 'delighted at being a great-grandmother', as she noted next day.

Nor did the old lady leave until nearly midnight when the crowds, though diminishing, were still singing and cheering; a police car with a loudspeaker vainly begged the rejoicing throng, 'Ladies and gentlemen, it is requested from the Palace that we have a little quietness, if you please.' Presently Michael Parker and another aide walked across the forecourt and said through the railings 'Princess Elizabeth wants some rest now. Prince Philip is with her, and there will be nothing more tonight.' Whereupon a voice from the darkness shouted 'Thank you!' and within a few minutes the crowd had dispersed.

In the morning there would be the saluting guns, the flying flags, the inundation of messages. 'We pray that the Prince will be a blessing to our Commonwealth and to the world,' was a typical cable from Premier Smuts of South Africa. 'The whole of Canada is elated,' reported the Governor-General, Lord Alexander. In far-sighted Melbourne, the town-hall carillon played *God save the Prince of Wales,* the first rendering of his lifetime. The next night the floodlamps in Trafalgar Square illuminated the fountains to play blue for a boy and, as Prince Charles has said, the ink has gushed ever since.

III

The bulletin put out by the Home Secretary differed in some respects from the first announcement from the Palace. 'Her Royal Highness and the infant Prince are both well,' ran the final phrasing. Within the Household there had been a flurry, in fact, lest the child should lack a royal title, and if he had unexpectedly arrived a week earlier, Charles would not have been born a Prince at all.

This arose from an oversight on the part of the King. Before becoming engaged to Princess Elizabeth, Philip had renounced his Greek royal titles and had elected simply to become known as Lieutenant Philip Mountbatten, taking his mother's maiden name as his own. Shortly before the wedding, however, the King decided that Philip should be created a Royal Highness and raised to the peerage as Baron Greenwich, Earl of Merioneth and Duke of Edinburgh. 'It is a great deal to give a man all at once,' he wrote in explanation to Queen Mary, 'but I know Philip

understands his new responsibilities on his marriage to Lilibet.'
To the King henceforward his son-in-law was Prince Philip,
although in legal reality an earlier decree by George V had
limited the title of Prince to the sons of the Sovereign and had
not made the style possible through a daughter. Without an
amendment, Philip and Elizabeth's son would be a Mountbatten
and at best could only use his father's second title, Earl of
Merioneth, as a courtesy.

Such was the advice tendered to the King by those versed in
such matters, and it was only on November 9th, five days before
the birth, that the King issued letters patent under the Great
Seal conferring on all children born to the Duke and Duchess
of Edinburgh the style of Royal Highness and the title of Prince
or Princess. The name 'Charles' – or Anne for a girl – appears
to have been submitted to the King beforehand for no other
reason than that Elizabeth and Philip liked it and wished to get
away from the run of family names. Unknown to them both, it
proved to be a pleasant coincidence that Charles had been the
name of the first-born son of Henry VII, the first Welsh King of
England, from whom the new Prince Charles of Edinburgh was
descended, by different lines, through all his four grandparents.

Yet the name at first remained secret from all save the
immediate family, and it was 'the baby Prince' whom the Palace
police went to see, two at a time, walking timidly into the unfamiliar nursery world inaugurated by Sister Helen Rowe and
soon to be firmly ruled by the nanny, Miss Helen Lightbody.
Nearly all the royal staff made their pilgrimage to the little crib,
while Sister Rowe or an assistant sat nearby with an anxious
'Do not touch!' expression.

Among earlier family admirers, Elizabeth's 'Aunt Rose' (the
Queen's sister, Countess Granville) felt that the newcomer
'couldn't be more angelic-looking ... golden haired with the
most beautiful complexion and amazingly delicate features for
so young a baby.' Looking through old photographs for a family
likeness, Queen Mary found an unexpected resemblance to the

Prince Consort, while Prince Philip when telephoning Madame Foufounis, an elderly family friend in Paris, exuberantly described his son as 'bouncing with health and looking at present like a plum pudding'. As a prospective godfather, Prince George of Greece heard that the baby had weighed seven pounds four ounces at birth, 'every ounce a treasure'.

As I was permitted to tell in an earlier book*, Princess Elizabeth similarly confided her maternal sentiments to a friend in a highly characteristic letter. 'Don't you think he is quite adorable? I still can't believe he is really mine, but perhaps that happens to new parents. Anyway, this particular boy's parents couldn't be more proud of him. It's wonderful to think, isn't it, that his arrival could give a bit of happiness to so many people, besides ourselves, at this time?' In answering letters from friends, the Princess tried to tell each correspondent something to interest them personally. To her former music teacher, Miss Mabel Lander, for instance, she confided, 'The baby is very sweet . . . Actually he has an interesting pair of hands for a baby, rather large but fine with long fingers – quite unlike mine and certainly unlike his father's.' And with her sister-in-law, Sophie of Hanover, the Princess was soon in agreement that the baby's smile was beginning to resemble Philip's, more and more.

Invited to take the first professional photographs, Cecil Beaton similarly noticed 'his remarkably long and pointed fingers' and shared the young mother's interest and amusement at 'the remarkable range of expression, the looks of surprise, disdain, defiance, anger and delight that ran across the minute face'. During the photographic session a week later at the family christening party at Buckingham Palace on December 15th, Baron Nahum was less fortunate with his camera, for the sleepy month-old baby was scarcely alert long enough to taste a fleck of christening-cake sugar from his father's finger.

The baptism service was held in the Music Room, where the

* *Her Majesty*, 1962, reprinted in *The Married Life of the Queen*, 1970.

crimson curtains of the great bow window framed the wintry garden view. According to the Archbishop of Canterbury, Dr Fisher, the Prince distinguished himself at his first ceremonial by remaining 'quiet as a mouse' and quite unperturbed on receiving the anointment of water from the River Jordan. As the youngest godparent, Princess Margaret held the baby at the font, to present him to the Archbishop and give the names Charles Philip Arthur George. Princess Elizabeth meanwhile watched with concern. 'I have never had a casualty at a christening yet.' Dr Fisher later assured her.

With the King and Queen, the other sponsors included Earl Mountbatten's elder daughter, Lady Brabourne, the Queen's brother, David Bowes-Lyon, and the baby's great-grandmother, the Dowager Marchioness of Milford Haven, then in her eighty-sixth year. There remained two absent sponsors unlikely to give an actuarial guarantee of any vows they undertook. King Haakon of Norway, for whom the Earl of Athlone stood proxy, was then seventy-six, and, in his eighties, old Prince George of Greece, a most benevolent Uncle of Prince Philip's boyhood, ultimately felt unable to make the journey and was represented by Philip himself.

The final 'George' of the four names may well have been chosen to compliment this benign but ancient godparent, as well as the child's grandfather, George VI, and great grandfather, George V. 'Arthur' had also been King George VI's third name: the Celtic name which Henry VII, first Welsh King of England, bestowed on his son, and the family name of Princess Elizabeth's godfather, the Duke of Connaught, who had gained it in turn from *his* godfather, the first Duke of Wellington.

'The choir of the Chapel Royal sang gloriously,' wrote a guest, as well they might, for at least three of the boys at that time were the sons or nephews of royal choristers. In keeping with the intimate domestic atmosphere of these occasions, Princess Elizabeth's childhood nanny, Margaret Macdonald, was there, with the Windlesham Moor parlourmaid and Mrs Barnes, the

Windlesham cook, who had baked the family christening cake. Among the elderly guests, moreover, were four grand-daughters of Queen Victoria: Princess Marie Louise, Princess Alice of Athlone, and Lady Pat Ramsay, together with Prince Philip's grandmama, as we have seen, surely a unique quartet in the post-war world. All four, it seems, had themselves once worn the royal Victorian christening robe of creamy satin and Honiton lace which now graced the baby — as well as the King, Princess Elizabeth, Princess Margaret, the then Duke of Gloucester and the Princess Royal, among those present.

Some rivalry inevitably occurred among the old ladies to give Prince Charles a christening gift endowed with tradition, but Queen Mary clearly had the pleasure of gaining the lead. 'I gave the baby a silver gilt cup and cover which George III had given to a godson in 1780,' she noted in her diary that night, 'so that I gave a present from my great grandfather to my great grandson 168 years later.'

<h2 style="text-align:center">IV</h2>

With his name and title formally established, Prince Charles of Edinburgh spent his first Christmas at Buckingham Palace. Having mostly slept away the first weeks of his life in a cradle in his mother's dressing-room, the baby's first nursery was contrived amid the heavy chest-of-drawers and wardrobes of an overnight guest-room nearby. His Christmas room had a little tree on a dressing-table with twinkling decorations. The King was also at Buckingham Palace over Christmas, as he had been advised by his doctors to stay in London.

The Prince's nanny, the Edinburgh-born Helen Lightbody, had been seconded from the Duke and Duchess of Gloucester's household and, when the physicians relented and permitted the King to visit Sandringham with his family in the New Year, Miss Lightbody found herself in the familiar scuffed old-fashioned nursery which she had formerly enjoyed with her earlier charges, the Princes William and Richard. Her first employer, a Scottish doctor, had asked only that his sons should be 'kept oot of my way, girrrl'. The Sandringham difficulty was that Princess Elizabeth contracted measles and for three or four weeks could not come near her baby.

It was March before the Princess resumed her official duties with a tour, accompanied by the Duke of Edinburgh, in Scotland. Charles' domain was then a nursery suite of two of the sunniest rooms at Windlesham Moor, with a bathroom and kitchenette, soon extended to a third room for an assistant nanny, Mabel Anderson. Miss Anderson had gained her post by inserting a 'Situations Wanted' advertisement in a nursing magazine, and was one day to have charge of all the Queen's children. The daughter of a policeman killed in the Liverpool blitz, her family had returned after his death to their Scottish home in Elgin, oddly enough only just down the road from Gordonstoun.

Prince Charles' earliest memory is of a pram of infinite length with a pair of hands at the end, but probably this precocious picture belongs to a year or more later, when he was emerging from the trance of babyhood. His father used to push him around the Windlesham lawns in his pram; his play pen, too, was set by the hour in the sun patio, with his blue toy rabbit, if not the woolly blue teddy bear usually reserved for indoors. Toys were always limited to a few firm favourites. This was still the era of both food and clothing rationing, and the gifts that poured in from every part of the world were accepted and acknowledged but mostly diverted to benefit children's hospitals and orphanages.

Parcels of beautiful baby clothes arrived from total strangers, particularly from America, gifts that caused the Princess to glow at the good they would do. At one stage, sets of knitted jackets, bonnets, baby shoes and gifts for every imaginable infant need were repacked for distribution to every mother with a baby born on November 14th, and the Registrar General's department had the task of supplying eligible names and addresses. The arrival of a ton of diapers caused royal hilarity, but six parcels of duplicate layettes were held in reserve for the arrival of twins. At the W.V.S. headquarters, the Princess drew numbers from a bag to distribute sixty surplus cot blankets.

Through the summer months at Windlesham, Miss Lightbody would ceremoniously bring the baby down to his parents in the drawing-room after tea. The Princess would take him in her arms and walk around the room, rocking him gently, rapturously happy. 'Isn't he getting fat? Isn't he getting fat?' And so he was; it was family history that Philip had been similarly plump as a baby, though without Charles' look of a tubby Edward the Seventh.

At Clarence House, where the renovations had disenchantingly dragged on into a second year, the pleasant day-nursery on the top floor was one of the first rooms to be finished, complete to the eggshell paint, and nothing remained to be done except for a line of 'baby blue' around the mouldings. 'We shall never get in!' the Princess once cried, ruefully, when a visit revealed another phase of 'suspended animation'. 'At least it gives time to arrange the furnishing,' a friend had written consolingly. And then suddenly the house was ready and on July 4th – Independence Day, as Philip pointed out – the Edinburghs moved in. Always an expert packer, Nanny Lightbody had once transported the Gloucester nursery halfway around the world, complete to the last toothbrush, when the Duke of Gloucester had been appointed Governor-General of Australia. Now she brought over the scales and the bead-counting board from Buckingham Palace, and an old brass-rimmed fireguard, from the distant era of 'the two little Princesses' at 145 Piccadilly, which proved to be a miraculous fit to the nursery fireplace. Not that Mrs Lightbody's peregrinations were ever complete. The Edinburghs had been in residence only a month when the time came to move to Balmoral.

For nearly three years, until the transition when his mother became Queen, the third floor of Clarence House provided the nursery hub of Prince Charles' world. He inaugurated it at the crawling stage, with hand-lamps and telephone kept safe from his reach, and the era ended with his fervent interest in the mounted guardsmen passing below in Stable Yard, and his noisy zeal for blowing a toy trumpet and banging a drum. The eternal verities were Nanna's desk between the windows, the nineteenth-century ladies and gentlemen on the chintz curtains and chair covers and the glass-fronted toy cupboards. Nanna's chair was a cosy wing-chair beside the radio, flanked on the farther side of the hearth by a low nursing chair which the Princess felt might still come in useful. In the centre of the room, an inappropriate highly-polished Georgian pedestal table was covered with a sparkling white cloth at meal-times, and with a coloured cloth for play. It was perhaps Princess Margaret who suggested that Charles needed a table of his own and chose a child-size trestle table with two miniature chairs to be drawn up for companionable games.

If Charles only vaguely recollects this light, airy nursery suite, its atmosphere was successfully transferred to the Palace nursery overlooking the Mall and he remembers the pictures which were in fact transferred there. There were bright Australian and South African landscapes, a Duncan Grant study of a busy harbour and the famous picture by Will Longstaff depicting a perspective of Englishmen of all epochs answering the call of Drake's drum. There would be more pictures, more personal treasures in plenty, later on.

Meanwhile, the young Prince took his first steps in publicity. Before the lease of Windlesham Moor came to an end, a news-reel crew took family shots in the garden, a sequence that delighted cinema audiences. In October Prince Philip flew to Malta to resume active naval service with the destroyer *Chequers* and was absent from his son's first birthday celebration, but the Princess was amused to see that her one-year-old had a good press. Two leading rival Sunday newspapers had confronted one another the previous day with 'main page middle spread' features on Charles and it was world news that he weighed twenty-four pounds and had cut six teeth.

2   The Elder Brother

Prince Charles was precisely one year and nine months old when his sister was born at Clarence House. The old photographs capture his bewilderment at the unusual crowds walling the road as he rode out in the car with Nanny Lightbody to spend the morning in the tranquil grounds of Buckingham Palace. Princess Anne was born at eleven fifty on Monday morning, August 15th, and Charles was told by his father at nursery lunch that he had a baby sister. Exceptionally, he was allowed to get down from the table to be taken to see her. He is remembered to have taken 'a most watchful protective interest' from the outset.

Princess Elizabeth's close preoccupation that July had been admittedly in the marriage pattern of her intimate friend, Lady Rupert Nevill. 'First a boy, then a girl' had been the felicitous schedule traced by Anne Camilla Nevill's children, deeply to Lord Rupert's satisfaction, 'first a Guy', as his son had been named, 'then a girl'. Guy had been born in 1945, to be followed by a daughter, Angela, in January, 1948, taking her cradled place in the world ten months ahead of Prince Charles.

It was Princess Elizabeth's fond hope that the pattern would be echoed in her own life, and the birth of Princess Anne happily fulfilled her anticipations. At the christening service in the Music Room at Buckingham Palace on October 21st, 1950, Camilla Nevill was a sponsor, together with the then Queen and her nephew, Andrew Elphinstone; Earl Mountbatten and his sister, the baby's grandmother, Princess Andrew of Greece (for whom Princess Alice of Athlone stood proxy) and Prince Philip's sister, Princess Margarita of Hohenlohe-Langenburg. In the vigilant care of Nanny Lightbody and his Aunt Margo, an exuberant

Prince Charles watched at least part of the ceremonial even if he eventually had to be lured away.

Through a phase of a few weeks, the old snapshots and photographs suggest the dilemma of an elder child no longer quite at the heart of the picture: the dismay and rebellion, remonstrance and vexation, and yet his attempt to 'care for baby' also. Hard put to gain attention at the christening tea, he unerringly tried a small boy's excuse to leave the room, first to his mother, then to his grandmother and with more explicit determination to Queen Mary.

As a reward for subsequent good behaviour, no doubt, he watched the procession for the State Opening of Parliament a week or two later, firmly held on the plinth of the garden wall, craning to see his grandparents within the State coach and delectably blowing them a kiss. Nor was this his first sight of ceremonial. From the same vantage point, he had watched part of the rehearsal ride for Trooping the Colour and then the procession from the Palace for the real thing the following day. In March he had also taken his first steps in the diplomatic world during the state visit of President and Madame Auriol of France, when his mother had brought them up to a nursery tea of banana sandwiches and sponge-cake, an interlude greatly to the family-loving Auriols' liking. Charles made a happy impression. 'Unlike most babies, he wasn't shy,' said the President. 'He took at once to Madame Auriol, but seemed a little taken aback when he first saw me. Yet we were soon friends.' The little Prince was encouraged to say *bonjour* and made a fairly successful attempt, almost before he had learned to say 'good morning'.

Nursery visitors that same year also included Queen Juliana of the Netherlands and the New Zealand High Commissioner, Sir (Charles) Patrick Duff, who was brought up to the nursery after presenting Princess Elizabeth with a sheet of his country's new Prince Charles 2d postage stamps. The weavings of coincidence are seldom so widely separated in time, but when Charles' portrait again appeared on a postage stamp, this time in Britain on the eve of the investiture, another Sir Charles (Michael) Duff played host to Prince Charles and all the royal family in Wales. The two Duffs are quite unrelated.

Prince Charles' adjustment to his sister was indeed so smooth that the nursery staff recall nothing of remark from the phase. 'One's sister is just part of one's world,' Charles has said. Mabel Anderson soon had fuller charge of the little boy while Nanny Lightbody gave her attention to Princess Anne, the first baby girl she had ever tended. The elder brother's first memories of his sister as a separate individual are apparently of their voyage on the royal yacht *Britannia* in 1954, memories strenghtened by their innumerable photographs together at that time.

During Christmas, 1950, both Charles and Anne were at Sandringham while Princess Elizabeth spent the holiday with her husband in Malta. 'He is too sweet stumping around the room,' the King wrote to his daughter. 'We shall love having him at Sandringham. He is the fifth generation to live there and I hope he will get to love the place.'

The recollection Prince Charles has of his grandfather comes, however, from an incident shortly before his third birthday during a photographic session at Buckingham Palace. The Princess and her husband were absent on their tour of North America from which they could not return until November 17th, and Prince Charles recalls someone swinging a shiny watch and chain while he sat on a couch beside another figure larger than himself. The King's press secretary, Commander Colville, was in fact attempting to divert his attention from Anne and the present Queen Mother who were also in the room. But the pictures were successful, and again the camera strengthens the memory, for the photograph remains framed in the Queen's sitting-room to this day, blending a keepsake of her father as she last knew him with one of the earlier portraits of her son.

Queen Mary is more vividly remembered, probably owing to the regular visits the children paid her at Marlborough House. The Prince recalls the immense battle scenes commemorating

Marlborough's victories painted on the walls of the broad staircase, and because he perhaps correctly associated some of the costumed figures with the procession of Drake's drum in his nursery painting, the old lady upstairs with her marcel-waved white hair lost some of her vaguely intimidating qualities. His great-grandmother sat very upright, her feet on a footstool, and allowed him to play with the jade and Fabergé and other treasures which he adored choosing from her glittering display cabinets. But clearest of all shine the Prince's playtime memories of his mother, so difficult to disentangle from the thrall of love and constant fun.

II

It is well known that the present Queen seldom missed any opportunity in her well-organised day of being with her children, and still more was this the case in the more leisurely days of early motherhood when she was Princess Elizabeth, Duchess of Edinburgh. At Clarence House, Charles and Anne were taken down to her after breakfast every morning, and sometimes the nursery telephone would ring earlier when the Princess would ask from her bedroom, 'Would you like to bring Charles along now?' Not infrequently the morning playtime lasted until the Princess had to go out or receive visitors, and Charles and Anne often played at her feet while the business of the day went on around them.

After five o'clock it was 'Mummy's time' once more, except for friends and family. King Frederick of Denmark on one occasion brought a box of battleships, miniature replicas, for the nursery floor. Made of metal, however, none could float and the fleet lost favour after being scuppered in a bathtime ocean. At bedtime, the Princess enjoyed carrying Anne upstairs, with Charles clambering strenuously alongside. 'Say good night to John . . . say good night to Mrs McKee,' she would bid, if members of her staff were encountered. On most evenings she preferred to stay for the splashing and giggling of the bath, the young parents often bathing the children themselves when Philip was home. Queen Louise of Sweden once watched the romp, taking the customary seat that a bathroom provides. A group of ever-changing aquatic gifts were kept on a convenient shelf. Finally the Princess invariably came to the night nursery to kiss the children goodnight. Sometimes wearing a tiara, dressed to go out, as one of the staff has said, 'she must have seemed like the fairy queen of their story books.'

Visiting Malta in 1951, when the Princess dearly wished to take Charles with her and it was felt that conditions might not be suitable, her absence was skilfully camouflaged. Young guests attended children's matinees in the Clarence House cinema and Princess Margaret readily stepped in as deputy at bathtime or would come over from the Palace to see her niece and nephew tucked up in bed. When still not three, Charles was given the high responsibility of calling the garage for the car for the afternoon drive. 'And where are you going to take us this afternoon, Polly?' he would ask Mr Pollard, the chauffeur, in a grown-up way. A favourite drive was to Richmond Park, where Charles could walk and watch the deer and where, to Mabel Anderson's relief, he was rarely recognised or stalked by cameramen. 'I expect,' Nanny explained, when cameras pointed, 'they are trying to photograph the car.' The dashboard radio usually enlivened these drives and one day Charles abruptly asked, 'Please switch it off ... I don't like *Mrs Dale's Diary*.'

When official visitors to Clarence House heard the blast of a toy trumpet somewhere upstairs, they little realised that Princess Anne was learning to walk by pushing a large blue velvet elephant, stopping and starting to a trumpet blast in the style Prince Charles had recently seen at a circus. Shouldering a toy gun, he marched up and down the corridor, stamping his feet at each turn as he had seen the sentries do. When a valet emerged one day from his father's dressing-room, taking away some suits to brush them, Charles eyed him with deep suspicion. 'Those are my Papa's clothes. Where are you taking them?'

The grown-ups were often surprised at his eye for detail. He collected giveaway toys from cereal packets and once said with disgust, 'That's the third cowboy this month!' He could readily distinguish photographs of his father's frigate *Magpie* from other ships, a precocity conveniently dated by the fact that Prince Philip relinquished the command of *Magpie* in July, 1951, four months before his son's third birthday. Early mentors never tire of recollecting that Charles was always a biddable child, not lacking a decided will of his own, but with an inbuilt sweet nature that quickly softened any dissension.

Returning from a drive, he once startled Mr Holloway, the steward at Clarence House, by asking, 'Where is the Princess, please?' Not 'Mummy', as he usually called her, but 'the Princess' as he had heard others say. Told that she had gone out to tea, he was most indignant. 'But why?' he said. 'She knew I was coming back.' And when reminded that no doubt she had to go rather than disappoint somebody, Charles was instantly remorseful. 'Perhaps you are right,' he said, with precisely his mother's glance and tone of voice.

In more acute differences, spankings were rare, for a reminder that he would upset Nanna or Granny evoked deep and endearing repentance. Later on, Mrs Anderson cannot recall any occasion when it was necessary to refer to his father on any question of discipline.

However rueful Prince Philip may have felt on relinquishing his naval career, his return home was an unqualified joy to his son. The little boy was never lost for a question, and Philip unexpectedly always found time for answer upon answer. One day seeing him in ceremonial uniform, Charles was so full of curiosity about the purpose of his sword and the insignia of rank, and his papa so patient in replying, that Philip was nearly late for his Palace appointment. At weekends they would play ball by the hour on the lawns of Royal Lodge or Frogmore. The young Prince was also deeply intrigued by the drawing-table which let down from the panelled wall in his father's study and so formed an excellent roof for a make-believe house. On his desk, for a while, Philip also kept a toy grasshopper which could unexpectedly leap in the air. If the grasshopper jumped it was a signal for Charles to go, and he always obediently left on cue.

His parents were away on his third birthday as we have seen: they were in fact in mid-Atlantic returning home from Newfoundland aboard the *Empress of Scotland*. But he was gleefully waiting to greet them at Euston Station three days later ... and stealing the show 'with his wide-eyed admiration for the parading Mounties from Canada'. At Christmas all the royal family were together again at Sandringham, although it must have seemed to Charles quite normal when at the end of January, 1952, his parents disappeared on another journey.

On February 5th the King played with the children after tea, and their grandmother presently followed them up to the nursery to kiss them goodnight and to hear Charles say his prayers, as she was accustomed to do while the Princess was away. Next morning, too, she came to the children's room as usual, only there gaining a few minutes respite from the grief that all but overwhelmed her. The King had died in his sleep, Elizabeth was now Queen and within a few hours millions throughout the world knew that Prince Charles was heir to the British Throne.

III

The new monarch herself told her son of the passing of the King, in her own way and in Christian terms which she felt a child might comprehend, and at her wish the children saw nothing of the mournful last rituals. Charles was taken on his usual walk beside his sister's pram to visit the Sandringham kennels and watch the moorhens on the lake, while, on the farther side of the estate, the cortège moved down the road to Wolferton. Then, a week or two later, the nursery life at Clarence House was resumed as usual.

The young Queen – still only twenty-five – altered the hour of her weekly audience with her Prime Minister, Mr Churchill, from five thirty to six thirty to avoid encroaching on her early evening session with the children. As Heir Apparent to the Crown, her three-year-old son now bore the traditional titles of Duke of Rothesay, Earl of Carrick and Baron of Renfrew, Lord of the Isles and Great Steward of Scotland as well as the more remunerative title of Duke of Cornwall. Originating before the Norman Conquest and more formally created by Parliament and bestowed by charter in 1337, this ancient style was to lay the foundation of his life-long fortune, an inheritance spread from Cornwall to Kennington and in manors and acreages from the Isles of Scilly to forests in Gloucestershire and the handsome acreages of Wiltshire farms. But in the nursery the ultimate recipient of this avalanche of tax-free wealth and future responsibility was still Charles ... and under no circumstances was he 'Charlie', not even in jest, curiously enough, to anyone in the Clarence House establishment.

If, later on, his sharp childish ears heard references to *Prince* Charles it was a style similar to Master William or Lady Rose, meaning no more than hearing his slightly older cousin spoken of as Prince Richard or knowing that a favourite policeman was Sergeant Brown. A princess in a fairy tale was surely someone like his Aunt Margo, and pointed stories about young princes were seldom encouraged. A story is told of those early days when, chancing to find a private secretary sorting through papers, he asked what he was doing, a question fired off with every opportunity, and received the incautious reply, 'I'm getting these papers ready for the Queen.'

'The Queen? Who is that?'

'Why, it's your mother.'

'The Queen is my mummy?' said the little boy, with a puzzled look. The secretary told Diana Lyttelton that he felt he had made a gaffe, as if disclosing the secret of Father Christmas. But Charles quickly accepted, as naturally as any child, the sternest fact of life he would ever learn. The usage of titles and distinctions was mastered in his case with neither more or less effort than children learn their manners, and always with emphasis on the courtesy and consideration due to others. One day, when he was a little older, the Queen scolded him for omitting the 'Mr' in speaking to a senior detective, but with other rules there were also some relaxations. At his first meeting of the day he had always been required to bow to Queen Mary, and to his grandparents as King and Queen. But the new Queen felt she could not bear this increased daily deference from her children, and to that extent the formality was eased.

Meanwhile, Charles bowed to his 'Granny' of his own accord when he and Anne went to stay with the Queen Mother at Royal Lodge in the March of Accession year. In their absence, the superintendent, Mr Seymour, examined and plotted their nursery for transfer to Buckingham Palace as meticulously as a touring stage-manager might plan the move of scenery and props. The ultimate result was surprising. A box of toy soldiers still occupied its usual place on a right-hand shelf of the toy cupboard, and the cuckoo clock upon the wall was still exactly aligned with a neighbouring picture.

In April, indeed on Maundy Thursday, the family began their last day at Clarence House by giving a sitting after breakfast to Edward Halliday, the artist, to enable him to finish painting a conversation piece of the young Queen in her familiar sitting-room with her husband and the two children, a pastiche now charged with the essence of family occasions. Charles sits on the sofa with a book beside his mother and Anne plays with her building blocks upon the floor, while her father looks on with amusement from a stool beside the fire. Not very long ago, the Prince of Wales noticed the painting afresh at Windsor Castle and appropriated it for his own Palace sitting-room. 'It's my favourite,' he has said, with an affectionate glance at the two young parents depicted there, the baby sister and the intent small boy in white socks, a captive golden moment of childhood, a scene at the threshold of memory.

Around the time of the Palace move, Charles was also promoted to a new bed, boy-sized and modern, a bedstead of honey-toned West Country yew in the traditional Windsor style, princely in that it was regally decked with eighteen escutcheons of various animals in enamel and silver; it had been specially made for him by students of the Royal College of Art.

For all that has been said to the contrary, Prince Charles remembers little of his mother's Coronation. In his late teens, he went through a phase of curiosity about past family events, and looked over the old photograph albums, leafed through the remaining press photographs in the files and missed few opportunities to see old news-reel or television film covering war and post-war history. So much was already familiar, he found, that it became almost impossible to disentangle remembered photographs from true recollection. Yet he once recalled distinct impressions of seeing the stands erected in central London that transformed familiar streets into canyons of wooden seating.

The little Prince was present when the tailors were fitting the two velvet robes the Queen would wear during the ceremony, and he found it a good joke that any part should be called a train. With his mother and Princess Anne he went one day to see the renovated Coronation coach and he jubilantly entered into the spirit of the occasion, bouncing up and down to test the new rubber seating as Anne was doing and placing the pristine upholstery and gilded paintwork in more peril than any refurbisher ever envisaged. He visited the coach again with Anne when the horses were being schooled and enjoyed a trial run around the yard, a ride not to be experienced in his own right for perhaps another sixty years. Remarkably he had learned and remembered the names of some of the horses, Tovey and Snowhite, Cunningham and Eisenhower, and the veteran Noah, who was one of the gentlest horses of the Royal Mews and therefore his favourite.

While his parents and his grandmother endeavoured to bring within his understanding why it was that the Queen should ride to the Abbey to make her promises and to·be crowned, brother and sister enthusiastically played 'Coronations', dressing up, processing and pretending to make solemn promises to be good; but it was doubtful whether even Charles, though two years the elder, could be trusted to watch any part of the ceremony without fidgeting. At his first church service, he had been so voluble after a few minutes that he had to be removed. On the day after his fourth birthday, the Queen Mother took him to a children's concert at the Royal Festival Hall, his first appearance at a public entertainment, but he wriggled so much that within twenty minutes Miss Anderson had to take him out.

His birthday, celebrated on familiar ground with a children's party at home, was more successful. Fourteen other children, with accompanying mothers or nannies, were invited to the blue-columned Music Room; they included the Lascelles and Gloucester cousins, the Knatchbull boys, Sacha Phillips and her brother Nicholas, the two little Butter sisters, the Charteris children and, among the Nevills, both Angela, who was Charles' age, and her younger cousin, Rose, who was invited as the nearest in age to make company for Princess Anne. The big room offered scope for musical chairs, a marionette show and other diversions, and Charles was on his best behaviour, as always in an accustomed situation, gravely receiving his guests as he had seen his father do.

As the Coronation drew near, the adults agreed that he could safely watch part of the ceremony. He still remembers the barber coming to the Palace on an unaccustomed day to cut his hair and sleek it down with brilliantine. He saw his parents ride from the Palace in the State Coach amid the pageantry of escorting cavalry, and presently, dressed in a long-trousered suit of cream satin, he was driven unobserved with Mrs Anderson by a quiet route to Dean's Yard, and so into the Abbey. With all eyes on the absorbing central scene, few noticed when he was ushered into the front row of the royal box to sit between the Queen Mother and Princess Margaret.

The timing was felicitous. He arrived at the moment when his mother was taking her seat in the Coronation Chair, and the choir and orchestra were filling the Abbey with the joyous sound of the Handel anthem *Zadok the Priest*, and before long Charles began to ply his grandmother with questions. At one moment he disappeared from sight to retrieve the evening bag that had slipped from her lap, at another he craned over the edge of the royal box as if anxious to glimpse the gold plate just below. But he saw the Queen crowned and, for the most part, sat quite still and absorbed, chin in hand. After returning to the Palace for nursery lunch, the other indelible impression was when his mother, wearing her Crown, took him on to the balcony. The distant space, usually shimmering like a minnow pond with passing cars, was packed now with people, a sea of uplifted faces, cheering repeatedly in massive jubilant surges, no doubt the strangest sound he had ever heard, a sound to remember.

IV

In those days the royal yacht *Britannia* had not then undergone her trials, and the Queen and the Duke of Edinburgh undertook their inaugural Commonwealth tour in the adapted Shaw Savill liner *Gothic*. They were to embark from Jamaica, leaving London by air on November 23rd, nine days after Prince Charles' fifth birthday, and having reminded him of the responsibility of 'being good and looking after Anne', they saw him safely tucked up into bed. The Queen quite broke down afterwards at the thought of the months that must pass before she could see him again, but next morning, hand in hand with his new governess, Miss Peebles, the little boy went to the large geographic globe in the

Palace schoolroom to spin the blue of the Atlantic in the mysterious ritual of seeing where Mama and Papa would be.

Charting their route, from the West Indies to New Zealand and Australia, Catherine Peebles enlivened their progress with personal knowledge, for she knew Melbourne and Adelaide and had worked as a governess in Canberra and Hobart, first with the family of Sir Ronald Cross, Governor of Tasmania, and then with the daughter of Viscountess Clive, through whom she became known to the Duchess of Gloucester. 'Miss Peebles is such a nice woman,' wrote Lady Clive, in a letter of recommendation, 'very good at exercising a gentle discipline. She teaches children self-control and a sense of humour.'

On this favourable note, Miss Peebles had joined the Duchess of Kent's household to take charge of Prince Michael and Princess Alexandra. Glasgow-born, a brunette in her middle forties, she was then readily seconded to the Scottish brigade at the Palace. Her favourite maxim was 'firmness and fairness'. She started Charles right away on the Beacon Readers, and on Christmas Day, when the Queen telephoned from Auckland, he jubilantly announced, 'I can read!' Copying from his Beacon he was also beginning to write, with prophetic insight, 'Here is baby sister. She likes to play horse.'

'Mispy' – Miss P as she became known – quickly discovered an essential difference between the children, that the little girl could amuse herself, while Charles liked to be amused. 'He was very responsive to kindness,' she once wrote of her pupil, 'but if you shouted at him he drew back into his shell and for a time you would be able to do nothing with him.' At Royal Lodge, where in their mother's absence the children spent most weekends with their grandmother, Charles proudly owned a pony named William, later passed on to Princess Anne, on which he first learned to ride. 'Will you draw me tomorrow?' he asked the artist Ulrica Forbes, when she was sketching Anne. 'Will you draw me on my pony?' and when Miss Forbes obliged he promptly asked Mispy to have the drawing sent to his mother in a letter 'because she will like it, you know'.

Written in turn by Miss Peebles and Mrs Lightbody, the weekly letter or report to the Queen soon invariably contained a postscript in Charles' larger-lettered hand. The author of the first Beacon Reader, Mr Fassett, may take pride that one of the messages, 'I send you love mother', was Beacon-inspired. The Queen had told Miss Peebles that she wished to hear of the little everyday things, and the diplomatic mailbag contained news of Miss Vacani's dancing classes; a reassurance that a book of Bible stories, mislaid in the post, had been found; news that a visit to the London zoo had successfully attracted no attention and repeated evidence that Charles' own prowess with his drawing-pad was, in Miss Peebles' phrase, 'better than average'.

The royal tour was scheduled to take 173 days. Letters and telephone calls assuaged the pangs of home-sickness, but the Queen could scarcely wait to see her children and, before leaving Australia, Captain Aitchison of the *Gothic* heard of a change of plan. It had been hoped that the Queen could complete her journey around the world by cruising home from Tobruk aboard *Britannia*. Why should the children not sail outward in the new royal yacht to the rendezvous, bringing the longed-for reunion fourteen days closer? The vessel had been launched on the Clyde on April 15th, 1953; and a year and a day later, Charles and Anne boarded her at Portsmouth for her maiden voyage 'to meet Mummy'.

The ship's company had not anticipated that their first passengers would include a governess, two nannies, a quickly seasick small boy and a boisterous three-year-old girl. Most surprised of all were four sailors detailed to escort and safeguard the children in a rota on board. Miss Peebles had suggested that the newly instituted routine of lessons should not be interrupted, and so for an hour after breakfast Charles sat beside her with his books, a cushion on his chair against the grown-up desk. The nursery staff were recommended to be inconspicuous except at meal times and, his school hour over, Charles was released to his sailors, usually to visit some new part of the ship, with Anne in tow. The shipwrights fixed up a slide for the children and made extra toys, buckets and brushes marked with their names, mops and miniature lengths of hose. It was long the pride of *Britannia* that on her maiden voyage the heir to the Throne rolled up his dungarees and swabbed the decks barefoot.

Charles all but disdained a boat-shaped pedal car that had been brought aboard, but one day unflinchingly braved the noise and machinery of the engine-room, though holding tight to his sailor's hand. Up on deck, the questions seldom ceased. 'Why is the band playing? How do they make that noise? What is happening now?' Watching the Walt Disney film, *Beaver Valley*, he wished to know why dogs did not build dams. Taken along to the men's mess deck, he needed no prompting. 'Are you having a nice dinner?'

At Malta, where the children made the first landfall of their lives outside Britain, they stayed happily for a week with Lord and Lady Louis Mountbatten. They paddled in the rock pools of Gozo, and one day Charles was taken to explore the aircraft-carrier *Eagle*, gravely returning salutes and shaking hands as he saw his great-uncle do. On May 2nd when the Queen was piped aboard the *Britannia* at Tobruk he was dissuaded with difficulty from joining the line of officers waiting to salute her. The Queen fondly thought her children tremendously changed during her six months' absence, Charles really quite grown-up. At Malta, however, during a further interlude on the island, the close proximity of the saluting guns alarmed him. 'Are you quite certain they won't hit us? Will they stop when we go ashore?'

During a combined Services parade, a journalist noticed with amusement that the young Prince stood toughly to attention on a balcony while here and there the troops were fainting on the parade ground. At Gibraltar, where the royal yacht made its last call, Charles and Anne were taken to see the celebrated Barbary apes, and the Prince offered his peanuts with prudent caution, outraged when one ape leapt onto Mrs Lightbody's shoulders. But when the time came to leave, the children responded with dignified waves to the onlookers. Perhaps under the guidance of Winston Churchill's instinct for a State occasion, the royal yacht, on returning home, sailed into the Pool of London, whence the Queen and her family then sailed upriver by royal barge to Westminster Pier. Walking behind their parents, the children shook hands in turn with the welcoming dignitaries. And riding in an open carriage with his parents, through the immense cheering crowds, amid the exciting jingle and clatter of a Sovereign's Escort of the Household Cavalry, home to Buckingham Palace, Charles at five and a half was probably aware for the first time of the distinction of having a mother who was Queen.

3 Next the Schoolboy

I

In 1955 the Emperor Haile Selassie paid a state visit to London and was delighted when, during the table talk at the ceremonious Palace banquet, the Queen enquired after the progress of one of his grandsons at school in Berkshire. Prince Charles was then within a month of his seventh birthday, and the Queen and Prince Philip sought out every scrap of information that might usefully shed light on the problem of his future schooling. Only the broad outlines were clear as yet. 'We plan to send him to boarding school as soon as he is nine,' the Queen had told Signora Scelba, wife of the Italian Prime Minister, earlier in the year. Meanwhile, among private friends, the conversation was of pre-prep schools and day schools, governesses and tutors, and Miss Peebles would have blushed if she could have known how often the Queen praised her work and ability.

'Mispy' now received her own copy of the Queen's weekly engagement card to enable her to acquaint her young pupil in her own way with the scope and significance of his mother's day-to-day activities. 'I found your country on the map today,' Charles proudly told Mr Winston Aldrich, the new United States ambassador; and on being introduced to a Nigerian diplomat he mentioned with grave politeness, 'I have been reading about a boy named Bombo who lives in Africa. Perhaps you know him?'

Although Charles took his lessons alone with his governess, the schoolroom hours were only from nine thirty until noon at the latest, less than half the lonely stint served by Queen Victoria's eldest son with his stern and aptly-named tutor, Mr Birch. Mispy's system of rewards for diligence and good behaviour

32

encouraged an afternoon spent in the open, often on an excursion lightly buttered with instruction. As they walked down the Mall to Trafalgar Square to look at the nearby shipping offices, Mispy was a fund of information on Nelson and the great trade routes of the world. When they drove out to Richmond Park or Hampstead Heath in an unobtrusive old car, the royal chauffeur and Detective-Sergeant Summers felt that they learned a great deal themselves from the games of general knowledge played en route. Before a pantomime visit to *Dick Whittington*, they first retraced the steps of Dick and his cat on Highgate Hill.

The Queen wished friends of the children to share in these outings whenever possible, and so Charles and his cousin, Norton Knatchbull, were shown around the Tower of London by the Chief Yeoman Warder and, another day, thrillingly descended the escalators of Trafalgar Square underground station. If the governess felt that it might be tempting fate to board a train, the two small boys with their parents, as Miss Peebles and Sergeant Summers appeared to be, seldom attracted attention. Several young friends indeed occasionally shared these explorations, to the Science Museum and to Madame Tussaud's, where the Prince's first sight of the wax figures of his parents caused a prolonged fit of giggles.

Miss Peebles took him through a series of studies of 'children in history', both princes and commoners, in pursuit of the policy of acquainting him gently and gradually with his own separate position. 'Your difference from other people isn't something that strikes you abruptly,' Charles once said. 'You don't suddenly wake up and cry "Yippee". It's something that drips on you inexorably.' Through the wooden oriel window of the 'spying loft' in St George's Chapel, Windsor, he watched the annual service of the Knights of the Garter, and although his impressions of the pageantry of Church and State were soon forgotten, he had seen Sir Winston Churchill in the procession; Charles also has an abiding heroic memory of the great statesman on another occasion seated on a rock beside Loch Muick, a burly figure with a chunk of driftwood across his knees, explaining in his deep voice, 'I am waiting for the Loch Muick monster', a figure of sombre courage.

II

At one time, when he was smaller, Miss Peebles had felt that Charles had 'only a vague relationship to the external world', but now the scene beyond his immediate family circle became increasingly enlarged in her educational London sight-seeing, and gradually unfolded in visits to his friends. The niece of a court official recalls a Saturday visit to her Hampshire farm when, immediately on arrival, Charles asked if he might see the chickens, plainly feeling obliged to inspect something before being entitled to relax. This autocratic phase faded quickly. A pair of boxing-gloves were presented to the Queen Mother for him in Canada but, Prince Philip recollects, 'he got too ferocious, so I had to put them away.' More successful were paternal cricket lessons at Balmoral and the swimming instruction which the Duke competently gave his son in the Palace pool.

The 1955 cruise in *Britannia* from Portsmouth and around the northern coast of Scotland to Aberdeen, saw a landmark in Charles' young life when he first stepped on to the soil of Wales to build sand-castles and paddle in one of the quieter coves of, appropriately, Milford Haven. In the following year, the royal yacht similarly cruised to the Western Isles and, on both voyages, Charles' and Anne's public visits ashore with their parents gave no clue to the happy presence aboard of young friends and cousins, not to mention the endearing 'other granny', Princess Andrew of Greece.

It was Mr Giles St Aubyn, a perceptive Eton schoolmaster and former tutor to the young Duke of Kent, who advised the Queen and Prince Philip that he considered Charles would benefit by a term or two at a pre-prep day school before going as a boarder to Cheam, the school Charles' parents had finally decided upon.

It was all satisfactorily settled long before Philip flew off on his four-month (1956–57) tour of the Pacific and Antarctica. The choice fell on a private school overlooking the gardens of Hans Place in the red-brick residential region behind Harrods. Hill House, Knightsbridge, a friend reported, was the only school she knew where the pavement outside was washed weekly, the basement railings dusted and every window regularly cleaned. In mid-October the school's founder and headmaster, Colonel Henry Townend, felt pleasantly surprised and flattered to be invited to tea at Buckingham Palace. An Oxford Blue and a former athletics gold medallist, he ran Hill House School with the aid of his wife, a state-registered nurse who had charge of health and housekeeping, and the Queen quickly unearthed the intriguing link that Mrs Townend had been theatre sister at Guy's Hospital to Sir John Weir, the obstetrician who had been present at Charles' birth.

Colonel Townend was a strong believer in physical fitness, putting a particular emphasis on the health and well-being of his pupils, and each of the school reports of his 120 pupils featured their progress in games and gymnastics. The school motto drew from Plutarch: *A child's mind is not a vessel to be filled, but a fire to be kindled.*

Shy and self-conscious, Prince Charles was spared the usual trauma of a small boy's first day at school. The Queen proposed that for a month or two he should attend for afternoons only and thus join in the recreational activities much as he was accustomed to do in Betty Vacani's dancing classes. If there seemed hopes that this might avoid undue publicity, the Queen, Prince Philip and the discreet Colonel Townend were disappointed. On November 7th Charles had no sooner arrived in Hans Place than an enterprising press photographer recognised him instantly, chiefly because he was the only boy wearing an overcoat with a velvet collar.

35

Happily, his schoolfellows were oblivious of such distinctions. The headmaster told them that Prince Charles would be joining them, but emphasised that he had no special privileges. On the contrary, he pointed out, it was they who were privileged, because they were free to make their own lives, while the Prince was not. The average response resembled that of Lady Longford's son, Kevin Pakenham, when he came home to report there was a new boy at school, a prince. 'What is he like?' his mother had asked. 'Oh, ordinary. I don't remember.' Walking two by two through the quieter streets to the Territorials' playing-field in Chelsea, the heir to the Throne was undetectable among the file of schoolboys in identical russet shorts, open-necked shirts, and cinnamon sweaters. Other than the uniform, the unmistakable Hill House hallmark was that they all politely raised their caps if motorists paused for them at a road-crossing. The group of small boys playing soccer was found to include an enthusiastic Prince Charles when photographed by a telephoto lens, but he was seldom indentified otherwise.

More unexpected was his enthusiasm for wrestling, which enabled him to release a great deal of boyish aggression within the well-defined rules. Young diplomats, churchmen, army and naval officers and business men at the outset of promising careers have mostly forgotten that they were once pinned to the mat by the future king in a basement gymnasium. More publicly, Prince Charles made his first appearance on any stage that December at the Chelsea Town Hall in a school end-of-term show. It has since been thought tactless to mention that in those innocent unracialist days Charles appeared in a parody of the nursery rhyme now usually called 'Ten Little Indians', and when one of the Indians 'skated off to Switzerland' Charles – in a pair of ski goggles – 'skated' off into the wings. It was harmless enough. Hill House makes a point of 'educating the boy to be part of a world community' and in 'Prince Charles' year' at least forty boys of every shade of colour were pupils from the neighbouring foreign embassies.

After Christmas, the Prince also had a tutor, Mr Michael Farebrother, at Sandringham, not only to bring him forward but also to provide some fairly constant masculine companionship in his father's absence, painlessly imparting a degree of extra strength in arithmetic and other subjects during the miles they walked, bicycled or covered on horseback around the frost-bound Norfolk countryside.

III

'And what is his favourite subject?' Colonel Townend had asked Miss Peebles. She replied that most of all Charles loved drawing and painting, closely followed by history. On his first full day at Hill House at the end of January, 1957, Charles thus naturally found himself at a drawing-board with his new and enlarged box of water-colours, painting not without youthful accomplishment a picture of a black and red ship sailing under a bridge towards a brilliant blue sea. The theme was a favourite one, and as a present for his tenth birthday the following year, Lady Lucy Wertheim gave him Christopher Wood's gay and lively painting *The Red Funnel*, with its sturdy tugs and fishing-boats leaving harbour – an appropriate picture, as she had thought, for the young Duke of Cornwall. He adored it and it has hung in one of his rooms ever since.

Not that the happy mood was entirely sustained throughout that first term. After a week, he had to stay away for three weeks with tonsillitis, but despite this lapse the teachers of Hill House, who are all called 'tutors', reported quick progress in the Upper VI; and the women tutors, who taught the younger boys, noted his 'good, firm, clear, well-formed writing', his 'keen interest' in Scripture, his aptitude for history, and his sweet singing voice 'especially in lower register'. His report at the end of the Lent term mentioned that he had 'made a fair start' in Latin, showed promise in French, was good in geography and particularly good in reading, with 'good expression'. Only arithmetic came to be marked as 'below form average, careful but slow – not very keen'. But the Queen perused this part of the report with maternal fortitude: she regarded herself as 'a true dunce with figures, without coming to much harm!'

One Hill House tutor remains under the impression that Charles had never been in a shop and that she herself gave him his first lesson on 'the value of the various coins with his mother's head on them'. On the other hand, the Prince was in Hamley's toy-shop in Regent Street a day or so after his eighth birthday, changing a ten-shilling note to buy two packets of plastic modelling material. Of the use of money he thus had an early practical test; the shopping excursion was made as usual in a Palace car, indeed, unlike many of his school fellows, Prince Charles had never been on a London bus.

His next term was as favourable as the first, despite a second interruption by tonsillitis. This time the Queen's doctors advised the removal of his tonsils, and the operation was performed in the Buhl Room at the Palace by Mr James Crook of the Great Ormond Street Hospital. Charles asked if he could have the tonsils to take home, and they were suitably displayed in the nursery, preserved in spirits in a jar, until the novelty palled. In royally giving thanks to all concerned, the surgeon and nurses, Charles found himself at last with the theatre attendant, Jack Vernon. 'And have you seen many operations?' he asked Mr Vernon expertly, following up with, 'And have you any children of your own?'

Mr Vernon explained that he had two, and that his daughter, Maureen, was only a month older than Charles. At this the young Prince felt a regal gesture was indicated, and he volunteered, 'Would you like me to write to her?' and a message, 'To Maureen. Love from Charles' was written then and there on a card headed Buckingham Palace.

Charles came through Hill House with adequate testimony that he was 'tremendously observant . . . never cheeky to the staff

... a boy with some creative capacity, with a receptive and retentive mind as well as individual determination.'

His parents were invited to the culmination of his stay, a Field Day at the Chelsea grounds, and the Queen and Prince Philip with Princess Anne and Mispy turned up as a family group. The Field Day, the programme pointed out, was 'not a sports day but a demonstration of some of the games played daily by the boys', and Charles showed his newly-acquired prowess in such events as a lively session of 'handball rugger', a physical training display, and the school speciality of circular cricket, in which each boy bats for six balls, bowls six balls, keeps wicket for six and then fields in different places for another six.

In the fifty-yard sprint, Charles was lying fourth only to be overtaken at the last instant by looking an admiring second too long at his mother. There followed a spectacular gun drill in which a mock wooden gun had to be dismantled and hauled across an imaginary ditch twenty feet wide and back again, a drill that, as the Colonel explained, had been reduced from thirty minutes to seven minutes flat. A relay race and jumping by the whole school concluded the display ... and then, for the first time, Prince Charles pulled his rank by being allowed to present all the members of his class to the Queen.

And so, next, to Cheam, although Charles first had his baptism as a yachtsman, sailing with his father in the Dragon-class *Bluebottle* at Cowes, and after the racing the confidence of the eight-year-old novice rose briskly by being allowed to take the tiller with only occasional advice from his father. Boys often measure their progress by their first long trousers. An old diary of 1957 mentions that at Balmoral Charles first wore his kilt of Rothesay tartan. His promising Hill House French was strengthened by the arrival of Mlle Bibiane de Roujoux at Balmoral; she was to be French tutor and companion and, as a rule, only French was spoken at the lunch table by Charles and Anne alike during her stay.

IV

The Queen and Prince Philip's one free day together before leaving Windsor that August had been the Bank Holiday and, while Britain basked in the sun, they paid their only preliminary visit to Cheam, with both their children in tow. Although he was Cheam's foremost old boy, I believe Philip had never seen the school. The establishment of his boyhood had been the former Cheam dating from Georgian days in the Surrey town of that name, lapped by the red roofs of encroaching suburbia, from which – while keeping the name – the school had moved in 1934. Now it occupies an estate of sixty acres on the Berkshire downs, some thirty miles west of Windsor, a Carolean-style mansion set amid fields and woods. Charles took everything in his stride but was probably shaken to find himself introduced to two headmasters, Mr Mark Wheeler and Mr Peter Beck, who ruled jointly over the ninety pupils. As the royal party was shown round, Princess Anne peeked into open cupboards, sat on the unyielding two-hundred-year-old horsehair mattresses, and looked astonished at the under-bed baskets in which the boys kept their clothes. Charles walked round quietly, asking no questions, keeping his hands behind his back, in his father's style. To Prince Philip and the Queen the rooms must have seemed worn, austere and silent, revealing little of their term-time activity.

The Queen remembers that when they set out from Balmoral in September to take Charles to London and thence direct to Cheam he was shivering with apprehension, while she herself felt highly nervous. Her son was to be treated like any other boy, but no other boy had a trunk with a brass plate inscribed 'H.R.H. Prince Charles' or a much-admired plain-clothes detective. Detective-Constable Reg Summers lived for a time in a cottage in the grounds and marched with the crocodile of boys to church on Sundays; he was Charles' only familiar link with home. When the Prince began at Hill House one or two fellow pupils were already firm friends, but at Cheam a master recalls seeing Charles amid the bustle of beginning-of-term looking 'very much alone and very miserable ... and notably in need of a haircut'.

A first-year boy named Fagan initiated him into the rules: the seven fifteen waking bell, the rush for seven forty inspection by Matron and morning prayers before breakfast, the duty of waiting at table (based on a rota system), and the system of black marks, 'Blacks', which could involve one's own house and the whole community in personal misdemeanour. The school had four divisions known as Canada, Australia, New Zealand and South Africa. Charles was placed in Canada and added four black marks to its score in his first term, but also gained the house 114 gold marks for good work and good behaviour. Falling ill with a stomach upset, he confided to Miss Colishaw, his form mistress, that at home he wasn't used to such rich food! In the evening, after high tea, he had to clean his shoes and share in such tasks as tidying the classroom. The maths master found him still engaged in his chores one night when he should have been upstairs. 'I can't help it, sir,' said Charles, 'I must do my duties.'

For the first time, also, the young Prince became aware of his own peculiar social problems. The boys whom he liked were wary lest they should seem to be 'sucking up'. 'It's often the really nice people who hang back,' the Prince once said in retrospect. However, laid up with 'flu in the school sanitorium, he chummed up with another patient, David Daukes, son of a NATO staff officer, and the two were soon 'Dave' and 'Chas' in boon companionship. Dave was taken home to Windsor on one of the two days permitted for visits that first term, and Chas in turn was taken to see David's grandmother, Lady Daukes, at Sevenoaks.

Lady Daukes believed that their friendship owed much to a mutual passion for model boats and yachts. A craze for sailing model ships swept the school and Charles, not having a ship of his own in the games-hut, wrote home for a craft from his fair-sized collection. Nanny Anderson saw to it that Charles' toys should not be more pretentious than those of the other boys and his ship, when it came, was the smallest in the school.

His ninth birthday was his first without any celebration, other than his nine greetings cards. His birthday tea was deferred from Thursday to the Saturday and his sugared cake from the Palace provided exactly eight slices, including one for Mr Summers. Chas and Dave had now been joined by Charles Donald and Chris Wilson; the friends saw themselves as 'the four musketeers' and later on formed 'the granite wall' of the soccer field. Prince Charles, in fact, soon settled down. Life at Cheam was much the same as in any other prep school: the daily round, the swirling enthusiasms, and the ragging in which the Prince soon gave as good as he got.

By coincidence, at the end-of-term concert, Charles again appeared in a skit of 'Ten Little Nigger Boys' as he had at Hill House, this time for three performances, one for a parents' audience that included the Queen and the Duke of Edinburgh. '*Five little Cheam boys standing in the hall. If one little Cheam boy should answer mother's call. There'll be* four little Cheam boys . . .'

But heads were shaken lest the fate of the one royal Cheam boy proved too tempting for the columnists who had only recently been requested by the Queen's press secretary to reduce their flow of school gossip. Towards the end of Prince Charles' first year at Cheam there nevertheless came a dramatic news lead that made every front page in the English-speaking world. The Commonwealth Games in Cardiff in 1958 were to have been presided over by the Queen, but then she fell ill with an attack of sinusitis and decided to use a recorded message at the end of the closing ceremony instead.

At Cheam, Peter Beck invited Charles and a group of other boys to watch the ceremony on the television set in his study, and as the cameras roamed over the huge audience packed in the stadium the Queen's voice came over the air. 'I want to take this opportunity of speaking to all Welsh people, not only in this arena, but wherever they may be. The British Empire and Commonwealth Games in the capital, together with all the activities of the Festival of Wales, have made this a memorable year in the Principality. I have therefore decided to mark it further by an act which will, I hope, give as much pleasure to all Welshmen as it does to me. I intend to create my son, Charles, Prince of Wales today.'

Such a tremendous storm of applause burst around the arena that the B.B.C. engineers interrupted the Queen's sound-track. In the headmaster's study, as Dermot Morrah described the scene, 'the other boys turned towards Charles, clapping and cheering. Peter Beck, in the secret beforehand, was watching the Prince and saw the look of acute embarrassment that flashed across his face.' The Queen's voice resumed, 'When he is grown-up I will present him to you at Caernarvon.' Through the room echoed the harmony of the great crowd singing, 'God Bless the Prince of Wales'. And for the blushing Prince it was indeed the tangible moment when he fully realised the loneliness of his position and the 'awful fate' that lay in store. He was still less than ten years old.

V

The Prince of Wales remained at Cheam until he was thirteen and a half. For four more years, after that unique proclamation of his rank, he lived out the rest of his childhood until in 1962 he had reached the staid rank of monitor and captain of the soccer First Eleven, a disastrous season, incidentally, in which Cheam lost every match.

As a schoolboy, he made no more than the conventional educational progress, 'above average in intelligence, but only average in attainment', as Peter Beck summed up. He continued to find mathematics his stumbling-block, while his ability to write good and graphic English was notable, his Latin average and his French 'ahead'. But once beyond that first year, a much wider group popularly knew him as 'Chas'. Accepted into the life of the school, his fellows agreeably gave him only a spasmodic tacit recognition of his out-of-school rank. When someone gave Chas a birthday gift of a doodle-master, a then novel arts toy which could draw complicated patterns, the entire school followed the royal lead with one in every locker. Charles found an especially congenial sanctuary in the carpentry shop where, among other things, he produced a coffee table which Princess Anne still has in use. His drawings and paintings regularly appeared in the school exhibitions. A friend is said to have admired a painting at Sandringham, and enquired, 'By your father, I suppose?' Charles pretended to examine the artist's name, and replied, 'No, it's by Self.'

Outside school were all the unrecorded achievements of his other – home and holiday – life. When still only nine, he had been entrusted with his first gun at Balmoral and cleanly bagged his first grouse. From Sandringham he joined the coot-shooting expeditions on Hickling Broad with his father, of whom he is intensely proud and fond. Father and son stayed at the Norfolk Naturalists' Lodge and, on a second visit, when floods covered even the raised entrance drive with steely water, they put up at the nearby Pleasure Boat Inn, where the local farmworkers and marshmen played darts in the low-beamed bar unaware of the royal visitors supping in the next room. On Speyside Charles similarly stayed at a village inn with Admiral Christopher Bonham-Carter, who taught him some of the finer arts of fly-fishing for salmon and remembers that, young as he was, Charles made a point of punctiliously seeking out the landlady after packing his bags to say goodbye to her and thank her.

He was eleven when Prince Philip gave him a sustained series of driving lessons and at twelve Charles habitually drove a

Land-Rover on the private estate roads of Birkhall. He also began polo instruction with his father, learning the strokes in correct sequence from the back of a wooden horse. Normally, he rode well and, although not sharing Princess Anne's riding enthusiasm, one saw him at thirteen assiduously practising polo shots on his own at Smith's Lawn.

4 Gordonstoun

In the early May of 1960 there occurred a day of national excitement and family significance when Prince Charles enjoyed the rare privilege of special leave from school, a day when he felt boyishly grown-up and first played a conscious part of his own in royal ceremonial, a day to remember. As it chanced, it was the fiftieth anniversary of the day when his great-grandfather, King George V, founder of the House of Windsor, had succeeded to the Throne, but this coincidence had little to do with either the festive banners and decorations or the crowds that lined the streets and packed the stands. The occasion was the wedding in Westminster Abbey of Princess Margaret and the then Mr Armstrong Jones, now Lord Snowdon, and since Prince Philip was to escort the bride to the altar, the duty fell upon Charles to walk in procession with the Queen and the Queen Mother under the gaze of two thousand wedding guests and the concealed yet watchful stare of the television cameras.

Apart from the memories, vague as they were, of his mother's Coronation, Prince Charles had never before shared in an event of State splendour in the Abbey. He was not yet twelve, a boy in formal Highland dress, kilted and belted with a silver buckle, a lace jabot at his throat.

'You'll be best man to the bridesmaids,' his new Uncle Tony had said, encouragingly, and at the wedding reception Charles gravely made it his duty to see that the bridesmaids missed nothing in the way of ice-cream, jelly and wedding-cake. A month or two later the younger bridesmaids, with friends and cousins, also featured at Sandringham, in a youthful group bathing from the sand-dunes near Holkham. They shared a cinema visit to see *Pollyanna* – at which Charles acknowledged the doorman's recognition with a conspiratorial wink – and one wet summer afternoon the youngsters had front row seats at Drury Lane to see *My Fair Lady*, afterwards trying out Doolittle elocution for the rest of the week. On a rainy day the children went shopping in King's Lynn, when sharp adult eyes noted that all four chose a paperback, with Charles gallantly paying.

It was part of the growing-up process that Charles read the lesson at a carol service at West Newton Church that year. He was soon primed and ready to inspect a sugar factory at King's Lynn, watching the manufacture of beet and sugar in what may be termed his first solo industrial tour. Visiting a banknote factory with Princess Anne, brother and sister came away with fresh-printed treasury notes of their own. There were other less enjoyable landmarks, including measles, and an appendix operation involving a midnight dash to the Ormond Street hospital, which Charles still keenly remembered eight years later. 'I was sorry afterwards when I watched a funny show on the telly. It hurt so much when I laughed.'

On recovering, Charles took his father's place at one of the Queen's round-table luncheons while Prince Philip was in South America, and kept up his end of the conversation 'as a young man should'. That Easter of 1962 also saw another manly enterprise in a father-and-son expedition to Germany, with Philip piloting him in a Heron of the Queen's Flight to visit his 'Aunt Sophie' and 'Uncle George' of Hesse. This was Charles' first journey abroad since the 1954 cruise to Tobruk, and an unusual opportunity to meet on their home ground three of his cousins, Prince Guelf of Hanover, a year his senior, Prince George, a year his junior, and their sister, Freddy (Princess Frederica Elizabeth), who was then only eight.

This cheerful quartet were together again for a skiing holiday at Tarasp in the Lower Engadine the following winter. All four were of course first cousins and, since Freddy was seldom

47

absent, one perhaps catches a ripple of far-sighted adult match-making. Within a few years Freddy would presumably be a good-looking and self-possessed young lady. Philip was merely keeping the options open. And in any event, that first Easter visit was a convenient prelude to Gordonstoun, where Guelf and George were soon to be Charles' fellow pupils.

II

Future historians may well mull over the effect of Scottish schooling on Prince Charles' strength of character. When the plans for him to go to Gordonstoun were first announced early in 1962, a large and sentimental sector of public opinion feared lest he were being unsuitably thrust willy-nilly into the 'rough, tough horrors' of the Kurt Hahn system. 'He is a very gentle boy and has a very kind heart, which I think is the essence of everything', the Queen Mother had noted not long before, and some measure of public disquiet arose lest a tender, sensitive and artistic individuality should be crushed under the horrors of what was thought to be the Philip Plan. 'It sounded gruesome,' Charles agreed on this aspect of the spartan discipline.

The Queen first visited Gordonstoun with her husband just before Charles returned to his last term but one at Cheam. The world of school remained a mystery to her, on her own admission, but she had read the Gordonstoun prospectus and made enquiries as to the school's aims as a whole for the boys themselves: 'No intellectual life can be expected to develop if there is no opportunity and no desire to be alone ... A school must set itself a more difficult task than the survival of the tough boy, it must strengthen the delicate, not only on his own interest but also for the service he can then render his country ... Without the instinct for adventure in young men, any civilisation must wilt and wither ...'

In Philip's long-term view, one could only put the facts of

the situation to Charles, with judicious guidance. 'This is the situation you're in. These are the choices.' In retrospect, this parental viewpoint worked out, and his son had a satisfactory sense of being consulted. 'He told me the pros and cons, then left me to decide', Charles has recorded. 'I freely subjected myself to what he thought best, because I had perfect confidence in my father's judgement. I'm glad I went to Gordonstoun. The toughness of the place – that's all much exaggerated. It was an education which tried to balance the physical and mental, with the emphasis on self-reliance . . .' When Charles joined Gordonstoun, Philip again made a father-and-son adventure out of the occasion, flying him to Lossiemouth on May 1st in the red Heron and circling to give his young passenger a first glimpse of the steep roofs and turrets of the old school mansion.

Indeed, there were buildings that Philip had helped to repair in the inaugural autumn of 1934, to Charles as remote as the stone age. The posse of photographers waiting to welcome them dubbed the event 'a fine old maypole dance' but agreed that Charles concealed his nerves very well. Firm boyish handshakes for Captain Ian Tennant, chairman of the board of governors, whom he already knew, for Robert Chew, the headmaster, for Henry Brereton, the warden, for housemasters and other staff, and a finger-cracking grasp from the school's head boy or 'Guardian', Peter Paice. Fewer cameras were turned on Prince Guelf, whose father had introduced him to the school earlier that morning.

Since it was an avowed aim of the Gordonstoun regime to 'free a boy of the enervating sense of privilege', a fine irony embellished the portrait of Prince Philip that hung in the dining-room, nor could it have lessened Charles' private agonies as a new boy to know that the 120-ton school schooner, *Prince Louis*, was named after a Mountbatten ancestor. On the other hand, his allotted school house, Windmill Lodge, was new since his father's day: a starkly modern stone and timber bungalow with green asbestos roofing, embodying little more than locker-rooms and an austere dormitory with floors of varnished deal, the walls unpainted, the light fittings bare as the uncurtained windows.

On settling in Prince Charles found himself emptying dustbins with Prince Guelf and Prince Alexander of Yugoslavia. His Mountbatten cousin, Norton Knatchbull, joined the garbage brigade shortly after, and there were classrooms to be cleaned, garden plots to be weeded and the frantic rush while taking it in turn to wait at table. The Queen had giggled at the picture of juvenile domesticity on reading that the day began at seven with a wash and cold shower, followed by a morning run, 'the boys then make their beds, clean their shoes and do part of the house-work'.

Charles jogged round the paths in shorts and running shoes, but showed none of his father's zeal to excel in javelin-throwing or the long jump during the forty-five-minute morning athletics break. His own unexpected choice was the 'assault course', hand over hand along the rope over the water course, wriggling at speed through the swinging barrels, skills that years later took the sting from Royal Marines commando training. Other instilled traits also proved useful. Palace secretaries occasionally find Charles lying flat on his back on the floor, the Gordonstoun prescription for twenty minutes relaxation after lunch still sometimes practised. On table duty, serving thirty boys, fetching and carrying, Charles preferred to forego his own food rather than gobble it down, a discipline not unhelpful in the Navy.

The new boy quickly adjusted to the disciplines of service, already inculcated at Cheam and so not entirely novel. The Court corps or the royal rabble, as his closer friends and cousins were variously known, filled their part with surprising discretion, not over-playing their companionship. In making new friends, Charles noticed that, as at Cheam, the more preferable characters were slow to come up and make themselves known, whereas the more assertive characters 'could be seen coming a mile off'. Charles recollects that he at first thought to himself, 'What's wrong with me? What *can* be wrong?' However, after two terms, a fair circle addressed him as 'Charlie boy', a few of the less deferential or less stuffy teachers as well as his school-fellows. In two years the Queen could comment in small talk with her Cabinet Ministers, as Mr Crossman noted, that Charles had been young in his class in taking his O-levels. He passed in Latin, French, History, English language and literature but still had to grind on in mathematics and physics.

Sports seemed less in his line, despite his hazardous captaincy of the soccer First Eleven at Cheam. Gordonstoun preferred rugby and Charles was apt to daydream on the field. In a tackle, though he never hung back, he realised that opponents faced an irresistible urge to get his face in the mud. Six months after Princess Anne broke her nose in a hunting accident, Prince Charles broke his in a rugger scrum, a case of less said soonest mended. Among his seldom publicised individual projects, he shone in pottery, and the royal family were assailed Christmas by Christmas with white and blue marmalade pots, white and green mugs, brown jugs large and small, beakers, jars and other trophies. A vase of bold sunflower design won him a silver school award. Lesser gifts were barrel-shaped greeny-brown hedgehogs and, although early specimens suffered broken legs, a herd of six survived to be distributed one year to various friends.

In summer, all the attractions of the seamanship course, the Sea Cadets, the expeditions, the swimming and surf-riding were piled before Charles and Guelf. If the youthful joys of weekend training on the school's small craft at Hopeman Harbour were marred by sightseers, Charles pretended not to notice or took strategic avoiding action. With the help of his detective, the quarry was said to be on one of the two whalers, while inconspicuously occupied on the other.

In his first term, a memorable canoe expedition was made from Hopeman two miles along the coast and thence across the open bay to Findhorn. Generations of schoolboys had done the trip before, year by year, but this time the weather turned blustery; 'the rain sloshed down', one boy wrote, and paddling the one-man kyaks became 'a slightly desperate slog'. While the kyaks closed up and the master fell astern to keep watch over their safety, the exercise became adventurous, physically demanding and threatening. Allowing for wind and currents, the journey distance was doubled until Charles and other younger boys reached Findhorn exhausted, but also excited, pleased with themselves and talking without restraint. That small episode has strengthened the Prince in self-reliance and created one of the firm foundations of later popularity.

Prince Charles' subsequent adult experience in the Services was similarly sketched out in schoolboy equivalent, not omitting square-bashing, route marching, field days and other popular ordeals depicted with humour and self-mockery in his letters home. When Charles was fifteen, more lively yearnings for adventure crystallised in a training spell with a Gordonstoun group at the shore establishment of H.M.S. *Vernon* at Portsmouth, which resulted in some initial knowledge of anti-submarine tactics, diving and mine-sweeping, with a day aboard the mine-sweeper *Monkton*.

The Queen had thought it might do Charles good to be shouted at by petty officers, but the greenhorns were treated gently. In nautical terms, they slept twelve to a cabin, which sounds stifling, but the *cabin* proved to be a spacious high-ceilinged dormitory ashore. The Gordonstoun 'Activities' moreover brought practical human insights gained in few other schools and certainly novel for an heir to the Throne. On becoming a senior boy, for instance, Charles had a share in the coastguard lookout; he was roused from his sleep to climb to the lookout room and open galley for the cold, bleak night watches in the small hours, and he was primed in drill with rockets, breeches-buoy and other tackle. His visit to Athens as a fourteen-year-old to act as crown-bearer at the wedding of the young King Constantine fired an interest in archaeology, and for several terms he became involved with his school-fellows in a passionate quest for the pre-history of Morayshire.

The research involved the painstaking excavation of a cave in search of an occupation floor where the men and women of the dim past may have left traces of habitation. Convinced that they were delving into past ages, the diggers lit a fire to judge the caveman effect. The smoke dislodged scores of unseen bats from the roof, and the Prince and his companions beat a hasty retreat. 'It was adventure,' said Charles, summing up the activities. 'It was fun. And in our own sea rescue service, our own fire brigade, the surf life-saving, coastguard and so on, we *were good*, no doubt about that.'

III

Cause and effect. One enthusiasm led to another. At his Aunt Margo's wedding, Charles had been unforgettably thrilled by the Arthur Bliss fanfares echoing through the vast abbey, and in consequence began learning to play the trumpet in his first Gordonstoun term. It was something his father had never attempted. Within a year he made his debut in a school concert, and soon astonished his aunt and others by both singing in the choir in a recital of religious music in St Giles Cathedral, Edinburgh, and playing the trumpet in the orchestra, 'terrorising the inhabitants', as he described it later.

His confidence diminished during subsequent rehearsal of a Rossini overture: 'We made such an awful noise in the back row. It got on my nerves in a way, and the nerves of others.' The music teacher, Frau Lachmann, would put down her violin and shout in agony, 'Ach, zoze trumpets. I cannot stand zoze trumpets.' So Charles gave up.

As with the wedding trumpets, however, he was inspired afresh by hearing Jacqueline du Pré at the Royal Festival Hall as soloist in the Dvořák cello concerto. The deep rich sound with all the infinite variations of tone opened his musical sensibilities at a new level, and his eyes kindle with enthusiasm whenever the instrument is discussed. His decision to take cello lessons set a new problem at the Palace. Old memories lingered of an earlier exponent in the family, and therefore of an instrument probably somewhere in store or on loan, and sure enough a cello belonging to a former Prince of Wales, King Edward VII, was run to earth at the Royal Military School of Music at Kneller Hall.

The heirloom was newly strung and renovated in readiness for Prince Charles' eighteenth birthday. He was already progressing with tuition two or three times a week with Miss Ella Taylor in Elgin, and within six months was playing with the Elgin Orchestra, no mere junior group but a band of enthusiastic musicians ranging in age from the teens to the fifties. Their repertoire covered Haydn, Mozart and Schubert, and Charles remembers attempting Beethoven's fifth symphony, 'A wonderful experience, but I couldn't play with strong enough concentration.'

As so often with youthful experiments, his talents were perhaps dispersed on too wide a scale. After a Gordonstoun production of Gilbert and Sullivan's *Patience* in which Charles sang as a chorus guardsman, Dr MacKnight, the school doctor, cast him as the ageing Pirate King in *The Pirates of Penzance*, 'a major part . . . because he can sing'. Appearing in red tights and fierce black moustachios, Charles revelled not only in exercising his baritone voice but also in the buffoonery and comic business. The Queen and Prince Philip flew north for the show, reviving the fun of the Windsor pantomimes on the libretto being suddenly sharpened by its audience. 'We object to major-generals as fathers-in-law,' the Pirate King explained. 'But we waive that point. We do not press it. We look over it'. And in his song of surrender in the last scene, the audience rocked with laughter and applause at the lines: 'We yield at once, with humbled mien . . . Because with all our faults we love our Queen.'

Again, among the facets of personality, Charles found that the time he gave to choir rehearsals was richly rewarding. 'I once sang in Benjamin Britten's *Saint Nicolas*. I didn't appreciate it at all at first. After several rehearsals I began to enjoy it. The same, too, with the *Dream of Gerontius*. I now become intensely moved when listening to it. Singing in a big choir is marvellous. The

Bach B Minor Mass . . . there's nothing like it, the volume of the voices, the sense of participation, you're not just listening, you're helping to make the sound. But it's something you can enjoy only if you keep at it . . .' And other Gordonstoun boys had the impression that Charles often tried to do too much, not for enjoyment in itself but because more was expected of him than from other boys.

His stage career, if one may call it so, arose from natural aptitudes tried to their utmost. When all the successive plays at Cheam culminated in his title role of *Richard III*, he went to great lengths to get it right and spent hours with a tape recording of Laurence Olivier as the waspish Richard Crouchback. 'I must have been either incredibly good or absolutely appalling,' the Prince recollects. 'When I finished there was a stunned silence until the producer in the wings started some applause.'

At Gordonstoun his talent was first evident in the small part of the Duke of Exeter in *Henry V*, and for the Christmas of 1965 the English master, Mr Anderson, cast him as *Macbeth*, the play in which his father had once had a three-line part. 'My performance must have nearly ditched him,' Philip clowned. Yet Charles studied the long part as thoroughly and seriously as he knew, his ability to take pains and his persistence seldom more evident. The cast placed bets on how many times the voice of the prompter would be heard. The task of becoming word-perfect in rehearsal was allotted only six weeks, but all passed off well. Some of the boy actors shook with nerves at the knowledge that the Queen and the Duke of Edinburgh would be in the audience, while Charles assumed confidence as readily as he donned his beard and costume, and 'enjoyed it all enormously. I love the language of Shakespeare, rolling it off the tongue and trying to captivate one's audience with such wonderful words . . .' That he was gaining a genuine facility in words and their emotional effect on listeners was apparent.

Few cuts were made in the monologues, some twenty lines long, notorious among professional actors. Ironies perilous to any prince playing the Macbeth 'that shalt be King hereafter' were overcome by the sheer sincerity of Charles' rendering. The one amendment to Shakespeare's stage direction was to the final 're-enter Macduff, with Macbeth's head'. The Queen, it was decided, should be spared the sight of a gory decapitated head in the likeness of her son.

Prince Charles was now a school prefect, enhanced with the status of a study of his own, a cubby-hole in which much of the space was taken up by his desk, which was usually covered by a Stuart tartan rug. The walls were mainly decorated with ambiguous prints of racing cars that demonstrated neither racing enthusiasm nor mechanical bent, but only his eagerness to please the giver. There were no 'pin-ups', other than a frieze of birthday cards. Prince Charles' 'carefulness' with girls was proverbial, and the only woman he chatted up in the Elgin orchestra were motherly souls of over thirty. Not for him the pleasures of Pete's cafe in the town, where illicit cigarettes passed from hand to hand and a pretence of showing drawings of Elgin Cathedral or patronising the jukebox developed into hazardous conversation with the fair sex at other tables.

A choral group of girls from Elgin Academy took part in *Iolanthe*. When the daughter of a local solicitor threw a party for the cast, the Prince was naturally invited, but even on this private occasion a ten-minute conversation with a blonde developed into lurid headlines in *France Dimanche* and elsewhere of 'Charles' love affair'. 'I asked him what he was going to do after school and he said he didn't really know yet. And I said, "Well, anyhow, I suppose I'll have to curtsey to you," and he said, no, he'd let me off that for the rest of my life. He was a super dancer, once he got going. I hope he marries someone as nice as himself.' Double-page spreads, as editors say, were based on this slim foundation.

Gossip was risked when a score of girls from a most respectable school in Aberdeen were invited to a Gordonstoun dance: it would be 'mush for Charlie boy', but Charles was conspicuously

Mother and child.
(*Camera Press*)

The first salute: at Clarence House, aged two.
(*Keystone Press Agency*)

A very young airman on flying manoeuvres, 1951.
(*Marcus Adams*)

The royal family in Coronation year at Balmoral.

Above: Family resemblances are marked:
at Royal Lodge, Windsor, 1954.
elow: The elder brother: The Prince of Wales with Prince Andrew, 1960.
(*Photograph by Sir Cecil Beaton*)

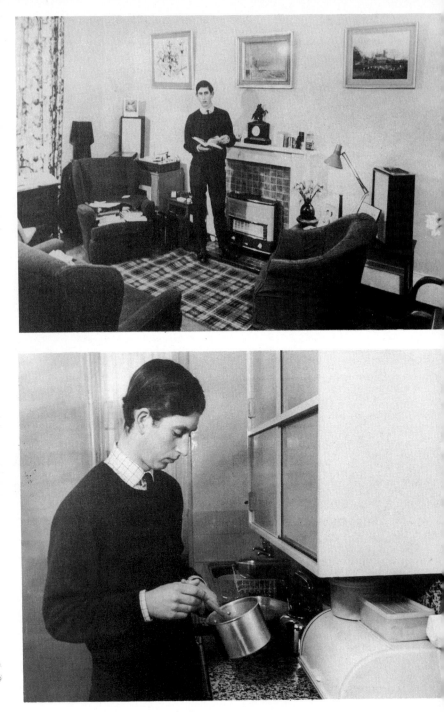

Above: Prince Charles in his study at Cambridge.
(Camera Press)

Below: The student Prince in his kitchen.
(Camera Press)

A little light patter: on stage in the Trinity revue, 1970.
(*Bippa*)

Oyez . . . A light moment with his sponsors, the Duke of Kent and the Duke of Beaufort, on introduction to the House of Lords, 1970.
(*Bippa*)

absent that weekend on a visit to his grandmother at the Castle of Mey. At one stage, a black market developed in name tapes pilfered from his spool in the linen room. Royal socks and underpants disappeared in the wash, and old boys of Prince Charles' generation suspect that such souvenirs are still treasured somewhere in the Highlands. A book of sonnets with his name, used for English literature studies, also vanished: Charles gave up reporting such losses. From such labyrinths of human behaviour arose dilemmas which no schoolboy could have foreseen or avoided. An exercise book containing his weekly school essays disappeared and a month or two later, incredibly, the German magazine *Der Stern* announced the scoop publication of 'four authentic essays by the Prince of Wales'.

The topics sounded promising: Prince Charles on democracy, on public opinion, on corruption and, in lighter vein, an essay on the four personal belongings he would choose to salvage if wrecked on a desert island. His highly practical ten-minute selection was a tent, a knife, a portable radio and lots of rope and string. The views on corruption, in fact, were not his own: editors could not know that he had been told to précis the views of the historian Lecky on the corrupting effects of power. On public opinion, the young author favoured the freedom of the press as a critic of the abuses of government, and championed television as the most effective medium for keeping the young informed and stimulated. On democracy, he deplored the tendency to vote for a party rather than for the personality of the candidate. Scotland Yard ran the original exercise book to earth via a Lancashire press agency from which photographic copies had been offered in Germany and elsewhere. But from America came stinging reports that the Prince had sold his composition book because his parents kept him short of money, a report of such utter invention that the Queen's press secretary issued stern denials.

The essay book had been stolen, of course, but the Prince still feels a sense of injury, less at the imputation of mercenary conduct than the implication that he would use his position to set a

57

false value on his schoolboy writings. It was like the cherry brandy affair all over again, that occasion in his first year at Gordonstoun when he had taken refuge from onlookers in what proved to be a hotel bar where, feeling called on to order something and in deep embarrassment, he had asked for the only drink he knew, the warming glass that occasionally appeared at shooting parties.

The incident might have passed unnoticed but for a woman journalist, who was aggrieved in turn when the Palace press office officially denied her story, an error worse compounded when the denial was withdrawn. A long-distance phone conversation with the Prince's detective at Gordonstoun, it turned out, had been misunderstood.

It was perhaps remarkable that the first Heir Apparent to go to boarding-school ran into no worse trouble. Just after the exercise book affair, headlines erupted when Gordonstoun staged a mock general election – at the same time as the real election that first brought Harold Wilson to power – and Prince Charles entered the mock arena as a vociferous supporter of the Scottish Nationalists. The Conservatives got round the cooks who served a pudding with the slogan 'Vote Tory' squirted across each plateful. Charles rallied Nationalist support by wearing a tartan rosette and marching up and down in his Stuart kilt, shouting 'Freedom for the Scots ... Scotland for Ever!' A Tory heckler reminded him that he was Prince of Wales and not Prince of Scotland. 'Freedom for Wales, too!' retorted Charles. 'That's for the next election.'

Though some of the speeches were tape-recorded and would have shown that the youthful Prince spoke convincingly with a witty and fairly well memorised text, the tapes were unhappily erased long since. A similar fate has evidently befallen the debates of the Sophist's Club, held every Wednesday evening at Mr Anderson's home. 'When he got up to speak, shyness and reserve dropped from him like a cloak,' his fellow student, Ross Benson, recalls. 'Even if sometimes illogical, his views were always clearly put. Authority would creep into his voice and his bearing.'

5   The Timbertopper

Like most young men, Prince Charles looks back on his school-days with a mingled sense of nostalgia and comic exasperation. He remembers the relief of escape at long last from school captivity and the regret, such as it was, of finally quitting the scenes of boyhood companionship. Yet before he finally left Gordonstoun at the close of the summer term of 1967, there was the eye-opening interlude in Australia in the previous year, which has never ceased to glow in the brightest colours.

As early as 1962, newspapers and spokesmen in Australia, Canada and Britain alike, had suggested that the Heir Apparent should spend at least part of his schooling in the Commonwealth and, like every useful idea turned up by press or Parliament – or indeed more directly in personal conversation or correspondence – the Queen had borne it in mind. While staying at Balmoral in 1965 the Australian Premier, Sir Robert Menzies, had found himself tactfully pumped on Australian schools and then asked to advise. 'I should be very sorry for the young Prince if he were at school in the middle of a crowded city in Australia, with people gazing at him, trying to get pictures of him, making him a raree-show,' Menzies had later set down his viewpoint. At Windsor Castle, one of the Queen's more frequent dinner guests was the Dean of Windsor, Dr Robin Woods, whose brother was Archbishop of Melbourne. And so attention rapidly focused on Geelong Grammar School some thirty miles from Melbourne, and in particular on its outback branch, Timbertop, 110 miles to the north, the wood cabin settlement of some 130 boys in the

region of gum trees and blue rocks on the lower slopes of the
Great Dividing Range.

If Charles had complained of the 'agony' of two more Gordonstoun years to go, he felt 'an instant enthusiasm' for what was
originally proposed as a pupil-exchange visit. A slight difficulty
was that the 'Timbertoppers' were younger than Charles, most
being in the fourteen to fifteen age group, but it was thought the
proposal might work if he were appointed 'a sort of N.C.O.' to
share rooms with another senior boy in the masters' bungalow.
An exchange scheme for an Australian boy at Gordonstoun could
soothe the abraded susceptibilities of other schools and, although
Timbertop offered no classes sufficiently mature for his needs,
Charles could experience at least one academic term, studying
alone with his books for his A-level subjects in French and
History, the latter particularly. After much discussion, a schedule
was accordingly planned that duly came stunningly true; then the
gulpy moment at the end of January, 1966, 'seeing one's father
and sister standing on the tarmac and waving goodbye, the
apprehensiveness because I'd heard the Australians were critical
... I had absolutely no need to worry after I'd been there an hour.
I absolutely adored it. I couldn't have enjoyed it more. The most
wonderful experience . . .'

His companions on the Qantas flight included Prince Philip's
former equerry, Squadron-Leader David Checketts, a one-time
public relations man now deputised as his equerry-secretary
'manager', and with Mrs Checketts and her three small children
and Detective-Inspector Derek Sharp, Charles felt that they
formed one happy family. At the first Pacific landfall, Honolulu,
a girl had rushed from the crowd to throw a garland around his
neck and plant a kiss upon his cheek, as if in welcome and adult
liberation, and out of the corner of his eye he had seen the news-
cameras and David's hint of assent. And not twenty-four hours
later in Canberra there he was, sailing on Lake Burley Griffin
with a pretty girl and caught up for the first time in the exhilarat-

ing sense of quick-change transformation that comes of transocean jet travel.

Leonie Tyrell was the daughter of a Government House secretary who had served for experience on the official Household staff at Buckingham Palace not long before – and Mrs Checketts observed with amusement the Prince's look of instant caution before accepting the invitation to go sailing . . . and his obvious relief on being reminded of the Palace link. Then he discovered that Leonie knew all four Sidney sisters – friends of his through the Nevills – whose father, Viscount De L'Isle, had been Governor-General until the previous year. He heard the news that Anne Sidney might soon be marrying an Australian. 'What shall we talk about?' Leonie had asked her parents, on being asked to show Charles round. 'Just talk about your friends,' they had advised, and only on reading this will the Prince probably discover how skilfully the adults had conspired to make him feel at home.

On February 3rd, Charles, David and Derek, as the group had become known to one another, arrived at Timbertop with more newsmen and photographers than there were schoolboys. But this was one of many bargains discreetly struck by David Checketts. In return for being free to follow Charles everywhere as he explored the grounds and woods and sheds and chalets, posing beside tractors and pig-sties and at fly-stands and wood-chopping blocks, the invaders were then honour-bound to leave the Prince undisturbed for the rest of the term. They kept their word, and Checketts was able to settle with his family into Devon Farm, a lush country estate on the outskirts of Melbourne, where he issued news bulletins as necessary, handled press enquiries and quietly offered Charles a home at free weekends. One news event not officially dealt with was that Mrs Checketts presented her husband with another daughter while they were there, much to Prince Charles' delight. On first hearing the news at Timbertop, he asked to be kept informed of the mother's progress and, as soon as convenient, he took a day off with his camera to take the first photographs of the baby, Snowdon-style, and sent the results home to the Queen in packages marked with red ink, 'Exclusive Pictures'. His mother returned his fire with her own latest snapshots of Prince Andrew and Prince Edward, aged six and two, the two small brothers of whom the Prince had affectionately said he could never see enough pictures while he was away.

II

On the 'all quiet' morning after his arrival at Timbertop the pommy Prince was introduced to one of the direst features of the Geelong outpost, the twice-weekly cross-country run through the bush, 'absolutely horrifying', as Charles summed up. 'It was ninety in the shade, with flies everywhere, dust and everything dry and brown. One ran, staggered, stumbled on.' But if this seemed 'more rigorous and tougher by far than Gordonstoun', the Prince was also prepared to find good in everything. Even the run, he wrote, 'makes you reasonably fit to go on expeditions over the weekends.' In the first week, too, like a new-landed immigrant from one of the old convict ships, he was sent out to chop up logs, 'on a hillside in boiling hot weather. I could hardly see my hands for blisters after that.' There were also jobs, such as 'cleaning out fly-traps, revolting glass bowls seething with flies and very ancient meat' and other unexpected disciplines and diversions, all providing material for an essay, 'Beating About the Bush', which Charles subsequently contributed to the Gordonstoun school magazine:

'Walking through the bush, you can't see anything except gum tree upon gum tree, which tends to become rather monotonous . . . When choosing a camp site you have to be careful where you put your tent, as a certain kind of gum tree sheds its branches without warning . . . You have to inspect every inch of ground you hope to put your tent on in case there are ants or other ghastly creatures. One species called Bull Ants, three-quarters of an inch long or more, bite like mad!

'Some boys manage to walk fantastic distances over a weekend of four days or less, and do 130 or even 200 miles. The furthest I've been is 60-70 miles in three days, climbing about five peaks on the way. At the camp site the cooking is done on an open fire in a trench. You have to be careful in hot weather that you don't start a bush fire. At the beginning of this term there was a total fire ban in force, so that you ate all tinned food cold.'

Nor was this lively account in any way a youthful exaggeration. When David Checketts joined in one weekend, he found himself walking forty miles, scrambling over successive ridges in the mountains and climbing several thousand feet.

Between these out-door tests of toughness and reliability, Charles shared a room with the only other senior boy, a sheep-farmer's son named Stuart Macgregor, where both worked quietly at their studies. There was little 'mickey-taking' from other boys, as Charles remembers. Taking dormitory duty one evening, he walked across the open in a heavy shower with an umbrella. 'They looked quizzically at this strange English thing,' he re-collects joyously. 'And as I walked out, having turned the lights off, there were shouts of "Oh, pommy bastard!" It was marvellous.'

At mid-term the two seniors side-stepped the bush marching with an expedition of their own, motoring down to Melbourne to see the Checketts and visit an exhibition of paintings by Sidney Nolan. Another weekend exeat was allowed for Charles to meet the Queen Mother when she visited Australia for an arts festival. Grandson and granny laughed at the incongruity of meeting one another in the middle of miles of tarmac, and were highly amused when the crowd seemed to applaud the enthusiastic kiss Charles planted on his grandmother's cheek. The following week the Palace mail was enlivened with photographs of their car trip together through the Snowy Mountains and the cottage they had shared at River Bend.

There were visits to sheep stations, where Charles demonstrated his lack of skill and, as he said, 'made a mess of it and left a somewhat shredded sheep', and some unrewarding experiments in gold-panning. Enquiring strangers at the school were usually discreetly told that the Prince had gone away fishing. It was true enough that he wandered away when he could with Inspector Derek Sharp to test his rod in some of the fascinating streams in the forest, not omitting excuses to his tutor afterwards if an essay had been neglected.

By Easter Charles was already launching the idea that he should stay a second term. Before the decision could be taken, Timbertop excelled itself by offering him the greatest adventure he had known to date. A tradition had sprung up that a party of thirty Geelong boys should annually visit the missionary stations in Papua and New Guinea administered by Australia, and in 1966 the event was brought forward to enable Charles to participate so that the native tribesmen might see 'the Great Son of the Queen'.

The schoolboys flew to Port Moresby and later sailed by the Anglican Mission launch to Dogura, where thousands of people had lined up on the beach to welcome the Prince; nurses, missionaries, primitives in tree bark skirts and native women decked in flowers and seashells. 'All waited with great dignity,' one visitor noted. 'There was no pressing forward for a better view, and the air was electric with excitement.'

With dramatic timing, Charles and his fellows landed in the light of the setting sun, and a great cry of greeting went up as he was led forward by the hand. During the next few days, his Timbertop training stood him in good stead, as he shook thousands of hands, hiked through the jungle, waded rivers not immune from leeches and crocodiles, downed mysterious liquid concoctions at native feasts and was then rightly decked with necklaces of dogs' teeth as a symbol of courage. Among messages home, he announced that he had been dished up to the oldest living cannibal. 'I kept my hands behind my back but he has lost his taste for humans.'

Some of the younger generation, the Prince noticed, appeared to be losing their age-old skills. 'I was given one or two presents by young people, and when I asked if they had made them they said their mothers or aunts had.' One festive evening he watched dancers, as he noted, 'in magnificent head-dresses of bird of paradise feathers, cassowary feathers, hornbill beaks and chicken feathers' and then joined in, with his party, contributing 'a somewhat hilarious reel'.

But above all, as he wrote later, he felt himself stirred by the unsullied, unsophisticated quality of new-found Christianity. 'How fresh and sincere I found the Ministry... Everyone was so eager to take part, the singing was almost deafening. One felt that it might almost be the original Church. Where Christianity is new it must be much easier to enter into the whole spirit of it whole-heartedly.'

III

Within the simple brick walls of Dogura Cathedral, Prince Charles had in fact found an ultimate unravelling of tense months of doubt, dissent and religious self-questioning, in a struggle which his earlier biographer, the late Dermot Morrah, has described as his most formative phase of spiritual development.

A year earlier it had happened that he was summoned from Gordonstoun a few days before the end of term to attend the funeral of his great-aunt Mary, the Princess Royal, who had died suddenly at her Yorkshire home. To Charles she had always seemed an elderly benevolent figure of another generation, and her funeral at Harewood on April 1st must have appeared in the light of a sad but inevitable order of events. On the following day, however, there occurred the death at the age of seventeen of his close and life-long friend, Lord Lewes – the Marquess of Abergavenny's only son – and the young Prince was flung into the most personal grief he had ever experienced. They had been more like brothers than friends, their lives so often enmeshed in the same domestic events, the same fun, at Windsor, Eridge and Uckfield. They had remained in close contact though at different schools, their correspondence winging between Eton and Gordonstoun. The Prince knew that Henry, who was nine months the elder, was ill with leukemia and had been planning to visit him in St Bart's hospital during the school holidays. And now no more.

As if in a bitter contrasting irony, Prince Charles was to be confirmed on April 13th in the private chapel at Windsor Castle, and the Archbishop of Canterbury felt that the arrangement should stand. It was a ceremony for which his charge had prepared with great seriousness. Charles had expressed a wish for 'my other clergymen' to attend, and so the chaplains of Gordonstoun, Crathie and the private chapel at Royal Lodge were also present. In a talk beforehand, Dr Ramsey found himself faced with questions on life and death put with youthful directness, yet still there remained the inward perplexities that neither the churchmen nor his sympathetic godmother, Princess Margaret, could allay.

Under such circumstances, it seemed more than a kindly coincidence that the Queen, with the Duke of Edinburgh, had long since arranged to hold the Royal Maundy ceremony at Canterbury Cathedral that year, an engagement sufficiently close to Eridge to enable them to pay a visit of comfort to their friends. At St George's Chapel, Windsor, it was noted that Charles became a frequent communicant, walking down from the Castle early in the morning on weekdays as well as Sundays when he was there. Some were reminded of the genuine and simple faith of his grandfather, George VI, while others also recognised that he was going through a crucial period of interrogation, perhaps more introspective than might be for his good. To give him the change at Timbertop was an obvious remedy, and the challenging Anglican service at Dogura was a culminating episode in casting out doubt.

IV

'The Prince happy as a lark,' wrote one of his hosts, soon after

Charles had returned from New Guinea and was visiting Cairns with David Checketts, intent on exploring as much as he could of the Great Barrier Reef. As if aware that he was taking a quiet new look at Queensland, the press then descended on him in droves. 'I think we happen to be public as well as private,' he said, posing good-humouredly for a cameraman with the eight-pound coral trout he had caught for lunch. Enjoying a few days at a cattle station, he spent hours one morning driving some twenty cattle back and forth between two stockyards to oblige the photographers, so that one reporter seriously estimated the twenty at four houndred head. Probably for the first time, he played polo in public with a club team at Goonoo-Goonoo in New South Wales. From Sydney he was game to try surf-riding at a carnival at North Bondi, but the beach show was no occasion for beginners and the opportunity slipped by. This deeply tanned and lively sightseer was by no means the moody, rather silent boy who had disconcerted his parents less than six months before.

If this second term at Timbertop seemed much a repetition of the first, his reading in history fired one of his earlier enthusiasms and he agreed to give a school lecture on King Charles I. As a small boy, the three-head Van Dyck portrait at Windsor had been his favourite picture, so mysterious and compelling that 'King Charles lived for me in that room in the Castle', although the romantic attraction of his namesake was not to outlast Prince Charles' later acquaintance with Cromwell, 'I realised that Charles I was not entirely splendid and innocent as I had always thought.' King Charles, 'the saddest of all kings', was to be Prince Charles' parting theme at Timbertop but, for the present, events more happily conspired for an international debut among his own youthful contemporaries. The Prince's departure from Australia all but coincided with the Commonwealth Games in Jamaica, and by way of leisurely plane stopovers in Auckland, Tahiti and Mexico City, he joined Prince Philip and Princess Anne at Montego Bay to play some share in the world's largest jamboree of toughly disciplined yet sturdily individualistic young men and women.

As Anne said, it wasn't hard work chatting up athletes. On the eve of her sixteenth birthday, she was still child enough to challenge Charles to collect more Commonwealth emblems than she could, and her brother still sufficiently boyish to revel in the 'hysterical' raft trip, shooting the rapids of the Rio Grande. At Balmoral, the Queen found her son bronzed and thinner and strangely taller, yet still there remained his last year at Gordonstoun.

In token of emancipation, Charles drove the car back to school in September with his six-year-old brother Andrew beside him in the front passenger seat, and his father complying with exact requirement of the law by being 'on or in the vehicle', occupying a passenger seat at the back. The Austin Princess carried learner plates to match Charles' provisional driving licence. As we have noted, he was of course a veteran of the royal estate roads, but it was not until April that he borrowed his mother's Rover 2000 and passed his driving test at first attempt at Isleworth; not bad, as the Queen felt, considering it had to be held in drizzling rain, on greasy roads, to the distracting slap and dab of the windscreen wipers.

On November 14th the ancient bells of the Curfew Tower at Windsor Castle rang a special peal for the Prince's eighteenth birthday, an honour unheard at Gordonstoun, where it was an ordinary day for the head boy at Windmill Lodge except for the early telephone call from his parents, the sheaf of birthday cards, the good wishes of his friends and a small celebration of cake and buns after prep that evening. In reality, the day held constitutional significance, for Prince Charles became of age under the Regency Act. Henceforward he could displace his father in the event of the incapacity of the Queen necessitating a Regency and, like the eighteen-year-old Queen Victoria, he could also reign without a Regent should he accede to the Throne.

More to the point, among the regal privileges of being eighteen, the Prince was also eligible to become one of the Counsellors of State whom the Queen empowers to undertake certain minor routine duties of state business concerning the United Kingdom – though not her other realms – when she is absent overseas. If Charles lightly pretended that this might bring relief from school duties, the joke misfired. In July, 1967, he was named with the Queen Mother, Princess Margaret and the late Duke of Gloucester as one of the four Counsellors of State empowered to act during the Queen's seven-day visit to Canada. But Prince Charles was then at the climax of work for his A-level exams in History and French at Gordonstoun and no duties arose.

Wincing under an impression that his schooldays were ending in utter tedium, he had to take the long view. In the spring term of 1967 he had gained the schoolboy accolade of being made Guardian or head boy. This promotion was not a gratuitous distinction imposed by his schoolmasters. The boys elect their own Colour Bearers, from whom ten Helpers and ultimately the Guardian are chosen, and Charles had passed through this selection process stage by stage until the post of Guardian became a definitive recognition of merit imposed directly by his school fellows. Not unlike the monarch, the Guardian had to see that the boys in general undertook their duties and in the case of punishment to grave offenders and other internal school matters he had the right to be consulted and the right to warn. When the headmaster decided that term that two offenders should be expelled, Prince Charles argued that they should be kept at school for better training and not merely turned loose from the school community. But the Guardian failed to carry the day, and had to swallow a rueful sense of injury to his ideals of fair play.

Friends warned Charles that he should not take things too seriously, as if all his life's training were not precisely directed to serious intent. The Gordonstoun authorities were just then preparing their 'Final Report to Parents', an unorthodox document providing comment not only on the standard reached in a pupil's studies but also giving judgement on his public spirit and sense of justice; his ability to follow the right course in the face of discomfort, boredom, scepticism or impulses of the moment; his ability to plan and organise, to deal with the unexpected, and on his imagination and fighting spirit. Whether a final report was ever despatched to the Queen remains unknown. Only the enquiring eyes of posterity may perhaps discover from the royal archives whether the 'degree of mental concentration', for interesting tasks or otherwise, included Charles' preoccupation with the cello and his forming taste in Bach and Mozart. In assessing his 'fighting spirit' and 'reaction time' Mr Chew, the headmaster, would have been unconcerned with his pupil's debut in competitive polo at Windsor that Easter when, scoring with notable dash and drive, he won Prince Philip's unstinted praise.

For the record his first polo trophy was a car compass, 'which everyone thinks I need', as he said with dry humour. At Cowes that summer, when Charles raced as helmsman for the first time, it was thought worthy of comment that the father was outsailed by the son. Prince Charles was loaned a Flying Fifteen *Labrador* while Prince Philip sailed in *Coweslip*. Charles had the bonus of Uffa Fox as crew and the handicap that his tiller extension broke just before the start, but *Labrador* nevertheless made up nine places and finished thirteenth, while *Coweslip* came twenty-second and last.

Meanwhile, Prince Charles had passed both his A-level subjects, gaining a grade B in History, with a distinction in the optional special paper, and a grade C in French, 'the sort of results' – a National Union of Teachers official asserted to the press – 'expected of a good, average candidate.' But Mr R. M. Todd, secretary of the Oxford and Cambridge Schools Examination Board which set the papers, also made it known that the Prince had shone in the optional history paper – 'the one which marks out the high flyers as regards judgement, initiative and historical acumen.'

6   The Undergraduate

In another and very different age, the higher education of an earlier Prince of Wales, Victoria and Albert's son, was settled at a solemn conference in Edinburgh by all those grimly taking part in his schooling. Shunning this unhelpful precedent, the Queen and Prince Philip had preferred, when Charles was seventeen, to give a dinner party for eight in the festive yet practical atmosphere of the evening but one before Christmas Eve.

This was in 1965, six weeks before Prince Charles first went to Timbertop, and eighteen months before his last days at Gordonstoun. The guests had included the Prime Minister, Mr Harold Wilson; the Archbishop of Canterbury, Dr Ramsey; the Dean of Windsor, Dr Woods, and the then Chairman of the Committee of University Vice-Chancellors, Sir Charles Wilson, whose experience ranged over the fanes of Oxford, Glasgow and Leicester. Then there was Earl Mountbatten of Burma, primarily to speak for the Services, and Sir Michael Adeane, the Queen's Principal Private Secretary, who had briefed them all on the problem awaiting them for discussion after dinner. Prince Charles was not present, however, and the Queen remained a listener during the debate on the wisest future course of the heir to the Throne. The Queen was neither bound to seek advice on her son's further education nor to accept any recommendation, and the debate ranged widely, from the innovations of the 'red brick' foundations to the virtues of Dartmouth, Cranwell and Sandhurst.

At breakfast next morning, Charles learned that nothing had been decided, although talk had gone on until a late hour. While at Timbertop, he heard of the considered opinion that a university should come before Service training, a judgement he also greatly favoured. 'I felt that being in the position I am,' he was to comment, 'I needed as much education and experience as possible.' He added his more personal view that it would be 'marvellous to have three years when you are not bound by anything, are not married and haven't got a particular job.' Later on, with plenty of time, there would be the Services to give one 'experience and responsibility, of life, of discipline, and above all of people and how to deal with people, to discipline them and be disciplined by them.'

Fair enough. His cousins, the Gloucesters, Prince Richard especially, had already given him some insight into Cambridge, 'the architectural glory of the place', the beauty of King's College Chapel which brought a lump to his throat, the sense of buildings 'revelling in their age'. Trinity was to be recommended as it had been his grandfather's college, it was of royal foundation and had a strong teaching side in history. Its fellowship was élite and yet three-fourths of the student body had come up from grammar schools, and Charles would have the new prospect of meeting and making friends among all manner of men.

On the Queen's behalf, Dr Woods first put a number of searching questions to most of the heads of the Cambridge colleges, nearly all of whom proposed 'that the Prince of Wales should have a special course and not risk taking a degree'. Whereupon Lord Butler, who had only recently been appointed Master of Trinity, expressed his own views with such forthright cogency that, as he recollects, 'such expedients were quickly abandoned and the Palace was weaned from a two-year to a three-year stay.'

'Rab' Butler had long been regarded as a kindly and practical family friend, and as early as the Christmas Vac. of 1966, Prince Charles had tea with him at Buckingham Palace, talking with youthful enthusiasm of his hopes of doing archaeology and anthropology at least for the first year, with the useful sequel that early in the New Year of 1967 Charles visited Cambridge with his father, from Sandringham. The avowed object was not only to meet his future tutor, Denis Marrian, but also to gain a closer acquaintance with the university and inspect his proposed rooms on staircase E in New Court. Charles was secretly delighted with it all: the secure and cloistered sense of passing beneath the ancient archway of the Great Gate of Trinity and finding, on its inner side, a statue of his favourite boy prince, the future Charles I; then the verdant expanse of Great Court and the leafy enclosure of New Court on the far side.

In this inner precinct his staircase in the north-west corner was the least conspicuous one, and his two rooms on the first floor still contained the scarred and time-worn furnishings rented from the college to implement his own things. The Prince was not gardener enough then to know that the twigs around the large oriel window were the promising winter outline of a rampaging wistaria. But what contented him best was the view, with a glimpse of the bright waters of the winding Cam, the spreading lawns of the Backs and the distant vista of the turrets of St John's.

'I wouldn't change a thing,' he said . . . although painters were busy weeks before he took up residence.

The Prince was to know the scene in every mood: the autumn woodsmoke that greeted him on his first evening when, at last alone, he leaned from his window, and the grinding note of the local dust-lorry that aroused him next morning. There was, as he wrote, 'every modulation of light and weather, like the orange-pink glow from the stone of the Wren Library in the last rays from a wintry sun', and there was 'the everlasting splashing of the Great Court fountain,' as well as 'the sound of photographers' boots on the ringing cobbles'.

But in October his arrival as a freshman in David Checkett's red mini was undoubtedly an historic moment of Cambridge history, and Charles has described his own 'distorted first impressions' with his own brand of humour. 'All that could be seen in front of Trinity Great Gate were serried ranks of variously trousered legs, from which I had to distinguish those of the

Master and the Senior Tutor ... If you have ever tried to get out of a mini you will know through what contortions you have to go. Having performed these in front of quite a large number of people, I was taken through the gate and into Great Court ... Perhaps the most vivid and memorable moment of arrival was when several burly, bowler-hatted gentlemen proceeded to drag shut those magnificent wooden gates to prevent the crowd from following in – it was like a scene from the French Revolution.'

II

Prince Charles is, I believe, the first prince in history ever to have undertaken a systematic academic study of his craft, of the primitive roots of awe and the deep human need of tribal leadership that upholds the prestige of princes and the majesty of kings. These elements of his profession all arose in his year of social anthropology, 'from the origins of man through Stonehenge to Julius Caesar', as Dr Glyn Daniel said. Charles also knew that he would ultimately enter the Navy and, 'I used to be teased,' he admits, 'by someone who asked why on earth I wanted to learn about Outer Mongolian tumuli, unless of course I was going to make a fundamental error in navigation.'

His studies involved the folk mysteries of Frazer's *Golden Bough* as well as modern theories of social behaviour. As he worked it out, 'if more people can be assisted to appreciate and understand their own social behaviour, the better and more healthy our society will be ... We should have a shrewd idea why we react to various situations and stimuli in the way we do.' There had been an occasion when his mother had felt hurt at some unwarranted and illogical criticism, and Charles in serious student mood may have sought to comfort her by the need of understanding, as he termed it, 'the conflicting dictates of human behavioural rationality'. If I know the Queen, she would have laughed at the gobbledegook, and laughter has always restored her equanimity. For Charles, anthropology not only explained something of his own role in the world, but also threw an illuminating light on Welsh and Scottish nationalism and on the problems besetting immigrant peoples. Threshing out difficulties with his tutor, Dr Marrian, two aspects of his personality, the goon and the enquiring undergraduate, flashed like the two sides of a spinning coin. He wanted to make the fullest use of his years at Cambridge, every facet of work and as much of the fun as time allowed.

Shortly before his twenty-fifth birthday, the Prince had occasion to look up his old archaeology and anthropology exam papers locked away in the Royal Library at Windsor. For the first time he came across his supervision report: 'He writes useful and thoughtful essays, although sometimes they are a little rushed. He is interested in discussion, and likes to draw parallels between the peoples we study and ourselves . . .' 'What a shrewd supervisor I had!' he once said. 'But I think it helps to illustrate the useful application of anthropology to modern existence.'

It suited Prince Charles' wry sense of humour that he cycled most mornings by way of King's Parade to his lectures in Downing Street. He revelled in being inconspicuous in the stream of cycling students, and became so lost in the flotilla that his detective, attempting to shadow him in a Land-Rover, experienced moments of unease in trying to distinguish him in the crowd. Two lectures a morning, practical classes for two hours each week, and an hour every week with each of his three study supervisors were the sufficient minimum. But Charles also preferred not to be cooped up too much within his rooms and spent many hours of quiet reading and writing in an alcove in the Wren Library. He also dined (or lunched) in hall more than the required five times weekly. The portrait of King Henry VIII straddled above the dons' table, aloof on their dais, while the potential King Charles III of the future sat on one of the long, hard benches at the scrubbed tables in the body of the hall, elbow to elbow with whoever chanced to be his neighbour, the unbarbered as well as the prim. Friendships struck up at table were, however, difficult to keep up, as he told Lord Butler. One couldn't be sure of ever finding the same neighbours again.

Denis Marrian and his wife gave student buffet lunches once a week in his own rooms up a stone staircase in Nevile's Court; Mrs Marrian, Director of Medical Studies at Girton, found that a social balance of two Girton girls to eight boys 'seemed about right'. Repetitious boy-and-girl invitations were avoided, and Dr Marrian had a stock proverb for the lovesick: 'Never run after a girl or a bus. There's always another one around the corner.' The coffee house opposite Trinity, the Whim-at-Eleven, irreverently became known as 'Him-at-Eleven' when Charles and friends were seen sampling the uniquely crisp doughnuts. One of the girls in the ever varying group considered him 'socially a clever clown although he draws one out.' When he joined the Dryden Dramatic Society, at first just to take part in the play-reading, a woman member thought him 'young for his age, though pretty confident'.

Lord Butler privately found it regrettable that the Prince's cronies 'tended to be conventional hunting and shooting types', yet Charles fraternised as widely as possible. Trinity men lightly called E stairway 'the Welsh staircase'. Excluding the Prince of Wales, three Welsh names featured among the eleven on the name-board, no more than a fair average. But in quality the shaggy-maned loquacious Welshman in No. 1 on the ground floor was the gifted president of the Trinity Student Union, Hywel Jones, destined to gain a brilliant First in economics.

H.R.H. in E6 and H. G. Jones in E1 seemed unlikely neighbours. Charles had been advised to consult Lord Butler on any point when in doubt, and at an early stage he asked the Master of Trinity what he should do about politics, probably with Hywel in mind. 'You know as well as I do, old boy, that in your position you cannot become publicly allied with any political group,' Rab Butler said. But it would clearly be useful to argue politics in private. The son of a Nonconformist minister from a mining community, Jones was conventional only in that he had read Karl Marx at fourteen and 'bummed around doing labouring jobs in Cardiff and playing in a rock group' before coming up, and some are of the opinion that Charles in the long run persuasively moderated Hywel Jones' views. The Cardiff youth came to regard his neighbour as 'surprisingly open-minded and flexible', and their equality as students soon concealed a friendship with understanding of each other's good qualities.

The Prince's intimate friend, Edward Woods, son of the Dean of Windsor, also lived on the next staircase, a strategic arrangement owing little to chance. The two joined the Madrigal Society together, and it was characteristic of the interruptions to his student career that Charles had to skip the second Society meeting in order to attend the State Opening of Parliament for the first time. It was an inside joke that the Duke of Norfolk made a family excursion of it that year, recalling not only the Prince from Cambridge but also Princess Anne from Benenden, to ride with their parents in the Irish Stage Coach. The occasion was Prince Charles' first full introduction to constitutional ceremonial and, as he sat in a Chair of State to the right of the Throne, the Queen's Speech ironically acquainted the Duke of Cornwall and Duke of Rothesay with her Labour Government's programme to abolish the system of hereditary peerages.

Two weeks later, in Cambridge, the bells of Great St Mary's rang a birthday peal for the Prince as they have done on the birthday of every heir to the Throne for two hundred years. The difference for Charles was that the heir climbed the hundred-old steps to the belfry to thank the twelve ringers in person and, for once, Cambridge townsfolk waited round about to applaud him. If the Prince enjoyed the illusion that he could usually move around unrecognised, dropping into bookshops, shopping in Woolworth's, it was because town and gown were polite. He went one evening with a club group to see the Marx Brothers' film *A Night at the Opera* and had to sign in at the door before being admitted. Charles wrote down his name as

77

Charlie Chester. 'I'm *entitled* to use that name,' he reassured the friend with him. John Malony, son of the Duchy of Cornwall Attorney General, and his companion indeed knew that the signature of the Earl of Chester was fully authentic.

In any event, Charles privately celebrated his anniversary with his cousin, Prince Richard of Gloucester, who was then living with four other architectural students in the penny-plain surroundings of Victoria Road, where they had decisively converted an unprepossessing terrace house into a triumphant tuppence-coloured renovation. Charles had first seen the house in its near-derelict state when Richard was at Magdalene two years earlier, and 'His Nibs' with Bernard Hunt, John Thomson and others of 'the gang' were in the first ferment of their ideas, gathering materials off demolition sites or snapping up such bargains as a £5 balcony. Now he viewed the result, a creative do-it-yourself experiment, revealing little to the street, but inside and at the back radically contemporary, from the plate-glass stairway extension to the Che Guevara pin-ups. Food for thought was provided that birthday, as well as burnt sausages.

III

For other occasions in the mitigation of university life, there was 'Doctor Ansell's house', as it had long been locally known, an old grey stone house on the Sandringham estate, now widely recognised under its restored name of Wood Farm. When Dr Ansell decided to retire and Prince Charles had first shaped his plans towards Trinity, it was seen that the place could be a useful retreat not only for weekends but equally in returning hospitality, on which the Queen always rigorously insisted.

While Prince Philip made drawings for replanning bedrooms and bathrooms and skilfully screening the garden, Charles had his fun in devising stereo music for every room, and an hilarious discusssion ensued on the merits of Bach in the bath and Strauss in the loo. Wood Farm was a long and narrow house built of the mingled stone and flint known as Norfolk rubble and roofed in the red Dutch tiles equally typical of the district. At right angles, close to the entrance of the drive, stood another cottage clearly useful for staff and housekeeping. A range of looseboxes won the Queen's eye and, though inconspicuous and secluded, the old farmhouse was but a few hundred yards from the royal stud at Wolferton.

Claim-staking became a family diversion. Prince Philip, strongly backed by Charles, visualised the house for a shooting party. Clearly it would become more pleasant and practical all the year round if Wood Farm could be used instead of opening up the 'Big House' for occasional visits. To begin with, it was overtly agreed that Charles should have first priority. No one could tell how he would react to the increased publicity of living in College. When his grandfather and his Uncle Henry of Gloucester had studied at Trinity, though for no more than a year, they had lived with protective official staff in a house leased for them off the Trumpington Road. Charles would not have sought even the creature comforts of a kitchenette, bathroom and telephone at Trinity if Lord Butler had not suggested these amenities.

The Queen inaugurated Wood Farm by spending a weekend there shortly after her son had happily settled into E6. The farmhouse had meanwhile been refloored and reroofed; some tall trees had been felled for security reasons and old farmyard walls removed, opening the way for wider lawns and a new sense of space. The dining-room fireplace had been effectively cured of 'smoking bronchitis'. On the walls here and there hung paintings by 'an obscure family artist' – otherwise Prince Philip —presently reinforced by one or two 'masterpieces by a young and vigorous artist of the new Norfolk school' and occasionally signed by 'Self'. Whether there was also pottery by Charles may be judged by the fact that in his second Cambridge term he joined the pottery evening classes at the town College of Arts and Technology, providing an unexpected bonus of personal interest to young local enthusiasts, housewives and sparetime craftsmen.

Prince Charles reported to Mabel Anderson that he had no time for anything, while in reality he energetically practised the royal precept of time for everything on a prodigious scale. David Taylor, the young editor of *Varsity* had asked if he would care to become a contributor, and the Prince's *First Impressions of Cambridge* duly appeared in the 21st anniversary issue ... with Lord Snowdon photographs on a backing page, as some noted with sardonic amusement. His cello remained in use both at Wood Farm and Cambridge, where he joined a local string quartet, his much-travelled instrument driven back and forth in the Land-Rover by Michael Varney, the Prince's detective, 'Odd Job' to the students. 'At night it was hard to ignore the timeless notes of the National Anthem or *Land of My Fathers*,' wrote Charles, 'punctuated by the melodious disintegration of bottles.' But one larky group also decided to go to his door ostensibly to apologise for their noise. They knocked and musical notes ceased from within. Charles came to the door, clutching his bow. 'I'm frightfully sorry,' he said. 'Did I disturb you?'

Inviting Lord and Lady Butler to dinner one night, he did most of the cooking, a goulash, which Lord Butler accorded, 'I must say was very good.' The Marrians, too, were entertained, and a dinner party which Charles gave for his director of anthropological studies, Dr John Coles, a Canadian from Toronto University, materialised into an agreed adventure: an expedition to visit the Dordogne for a few days at Easter to see some of the richest prehistoric sites in Europe.

Though not consciously so, this was also one of the few occasions of a princely gesture, for no other undergraduate could jaunt to France with his friends in an executive aircraft of the Queen's Flight, piloted by the Duke of Edinburgh. The Duke returned home the same day, while for Charles there opened another new dimension of acquaintance and independence. With Dr Coles, Dr Glyn Daniel, David Checketts and three or four student friends of his own age, he stayed at a hotel in Les Eyzies, sallying forth to see the reindeer paintings in the local honeycomb of caves, and the primitive carvings that so long haunt the mind. Driving north through the Loire, the Prince made a point of visiting the tombs of his Plantagenet ancestors at the Abbey of Fontrevault and, in Brittany, he examined the mysterious avenues and circles that are equated with Stonehenge. The holiday ended with a working weekend under canvas in Jersey, with the Cambridge Archaeological Society, meticulously sifting the soil with trowel and brush and humorously acquiring backache at the excavations in the La Cotte cave.

Discovering nothing more tangible than flints, Charles nevertheless found it richly exhilarating. And diligence had its fuller reward in the Tripos exams in archaeology and anthropology when he was placed in the first division in Class II. 'It will be a scandal if you cannot guarantee him a good First,' an important personage had said to Lord Butler. But the candidates, of course, worked under numbers, and the eight examiners marked the unidentified papers and only later looked up the names. A good result on merit, it was a triumphant completion of the Prince's first year.

IV

Charles had chaffed one of the Wren Library girls that he expected he would take a job in the Long Vac., and if by this he meant the job of being a Prince the forecast was borne out. He had planned as his summer project a series of visits to Government departments to enable him to gain a closer idea of some of the operations they sponsored, and thus take a bird's eye view of how government works. This was initially his own idea, one he hoped would be taken seriously, and he began with a visit to the newly-created Department of Employment and Productivity in St James' Square, although their conducted survey of graphs and statistics, a photo session and an armchair chat with Barbara Castle were perhaps not quite what he had in mind. He was happier visiting some of the Ministry's regional offices in Wales, sitting in – unidentified – with an interviewing officer at a Swansea employment exchange, touring the rehabilitation centre at Port Talbot and so forth.

Outside the Welsh Office in Cardiff, dissidents were out in force with Welsh Nationalist and Welsh Language banners. Smoke-bombs and eggs were thrown, to counter-jeers from more welcoming sections of the crowd whom the Prince startled by side-stepping from his group to ascertain for himself what the demonstration was all about. 'Well, I had slight butterflies,' he said afterwards, 'but I thought one could talk to them as perfectly ordinary people. One chap was holding a placard in Welsh, and I just asked what it meant. I hadn't learned much of the Welsh language then. And in fact he just hurled abuse and said, "Go home, Charlie". So after more questions I gave up. There was no point.' Yet the point perhaps was that the watching and now cheering crowd saw demonstrably that the Prince of Wales had guts, and the Prince discovered a little of what he wanted to know.

In those few weeks he not only flew by helicopter to a North Sea drilling rig, but also spent a morning down the pit at Welbeck Colliery, his first visit to a coal-mine. Wilfred Barrett, the colliery manager, decided to treat him as one of his own sons, and took him to the pit face to talk to men who were sweating in dirt and eating their pasties in dirt. 'He was just as ready to learn as my boys would have been.' Back in London, he descended into the clay tunnels of the new Victoria tube line, and was amazed and daunted that the digger gangs could work in so little space. In Edinburgh he talked to a newspaper editor and learned of the quick judgement and instant decisions that make up a new page.

At the Bankside power station in London he encountered the familiar face of another Trinity man who had taken a vacation job with the Central Electricity Board. 'That makes two of us, anyway.' And it was equally part of the Prince's own working vac. to undergo the ceremonies of installation as a Knight of the Garter, walking through the crowds in the full absurdity of plumed velvet cap and robes. The shouts this time were of 'Good old Charlie'! But the ceremonies of chivalry are to be taken seriously, with their prayers for steadfastness in the Christian faith. In the procession to the chapel there walked such figures of lasting history as Earl Alexander of Tunis, Earl Mountbatten of Burma and Viscount Montgomery of Alamein.

The Prince also attended Royal Ascot for the first time that year, and rode with the Queen in the traditional procession of open carriages along the course. The Ascot week house-party at Windsor Castle that summer was notable for its atmosphere of young people. Every young lady ever mentioned in print in some gossipy link with Charles seemed to be there as well as many who were sufficiently aware of the hazards of Fleet Street rarely to be mentioned at all. Sitting out with a friend, as Dermot Morrah observed, the Queen was amused at the enthusiasm with which her son sought out the prettiest partners in the room and inferred that his preference was already with the rosebuds rather than the sultry charms of the tiger-lilies.

In August, Prince Charles took his first R.A.F. flying lessons, going up from Tangmere airfield in a Chipmunk trainer for his aptitude tests with a young New Zealander, Squadron Leader Phillip Pinney. Six months later, after some fifteen hours' flying, he was recording his impressions of his first solo flight. 'I always thought I was going to be terrified. I was dreading the moment but because the weather had been so bad for so long I put in quite a lot more hours than is really vital. At the end of the runway, my instructor suddenly climbed out and said "You're on your own, mate," so there I was. I taxied and took off, wondering whether I could do it, and the moment I was in the air it was marvellous. No instructor to breathe down the back of your neck . . . ! I had a wonderful time. And fortunately I landed first time. I had visions of myself going round and round until the fuel ran out...'

It was all in the taskwork of being a Prince, the resolve and the effort, the tests and accomplishment, shaping, as his father had said, 'one step at a time'. This was now the 1968-9 season when, from summer until spring, Richard Cawston and his camera crews invaded every corner of royal life for the television documentary film, *Royal Family*. The cameras loomed over the breakfast table at Windsor Castle, over the barbecue at Balmoral, captured the gaiety of a Palace buffet luncheon held in honour of British Olympic athletes, watched Charles at his desk and on his Cambridge bicycle, and indeed awarded him his due share of screen space in a film that has remained etched in national and Commonwealth consciousness.

One remembers Charles explaining his cello to his young brother Prince Edward, and the little boy's surprise when a string snapped, stinging him on his chin. One recollects Charles and then Anne being slung in a harness from *Britannia* to an escorting frigate; Charles fly-fishing in Somerset; Charles asking royal questions on an oil-rig and getting royal answers, 'Er, what is a blow-out preventer?' 'It prevents blow-outs, actually.' The finished film, cut and edited, ran for 105 minutes and there are in fact forty-one hours of film deposited with the National Film Archive as a realistic bonus to posterity.

It was fortunate that the Prince had 'great powers of concentrating on his work', as the Master of Trinity noted. In his second Cambridge year he studied history, differing from his contemporaries only in that he retained his rooms in New Court, but henceforth there would always be interruptions. The film had only been in the early scripting stage when he flew to Melbourne with Harold Wilson and Edward Heath to attend the memorial service for the Australian Premier, Harold Holt. The cameras were, however, at work in the autumn when he again rode with the Queen to Westminster to take part in the State Opening of Parliament. It was the Queen's fifteenth enactment of the ceremony during her reign, and for Prince Charles his second attendance at his mother's side. Among private occasions, however, the film-makers missed his appearance that same month with the Dryden Society, cast in the Joe Orton comedy *Erpingham Camp*. Taking the part of a Services padre, Charles had borrowed a clerical collar from the Dean; the role involved him in having a custard pie thrust into his face and 'It's great fun,' he told Cliff Michelmore. 'Having an interest like that keeps one sane. In fact, when my small brothers heard a recording of the Goons, they thought it was me.'

The Prince celebrated his twentieth birthday without a ripple on his university life, but a weekend party at Wood Farm filled the house with guests, and it was a Cambridge undergraduate, Godfrey Argent, who had taken his birthday photographs at Windsor Castle some weeks previously. On the planning slate for the future were television interviews, films and radio broadcasts. But Charles was privately more concerned just then with another problem which he took to Lord Butler: whether it would be okay to appear next term in the Trinity revue. It would be a *Beyond the Fringe*-type show, Charles explained, 'full of the most awful groan jokes'. His adviser reassured him that in making public appearances it would be essential to know how to deliver throw-away lines. Accordingly, Prince Charles appeared in fourteen of the forty sketches of *Revulution*, as a singing dust-man, a Beatle-wigged pop cellist, and a conductor who had lost his orchestra, to name but a few, all good versatile spoof with quotable wit for the reporters at the preview. 'I must admit,' said Sir Cummerbund Overspill, as he escorted a pretty girl off stage, 'I must admit I like giving myself heirs.' But Sir Cummerbund was, of course, played by 'H.R.H. Prince of Wales', as the programme announced, and the final Sunday night performance in the lecture theatre was cancelled after protests from the Lord's Day Observance Society.

7   The Invested Prince

I

More than a year before the Prince of Wales had ever trod Trinity Great Court, the Queen had been petitioned that he should study at the University College of Wales at Aberystwyth. This petition was signed by 175 students, and the Queen agreed that they had a point. It would be useful for Charles to take a crammed course in Welsh history, language and culture, before his investiture or indeed before he inaugurated the new Royal Regiment of Wales as its Colonel-in-Chief. In family conclave, as Prince Philip said later, the Queen and her husband jotted down all the relevant factors; and Prince Charles was for every possible permutation of 'changes and challenges'.

And so on April 21st, 1969 – on the Queen's forty-third birthday – the Prince of Wales was formally enrolled at Aberystwyth for a nine-week term, which he already acutely knew would be a crash course in the art of skating through controversy. The petition had turned out to be the pebble that starts an avalanche. At the first hint of his coming, rival students of Aberystwyth and Bangor had locked themselves in their lecture rooms as a sit-in protest. Seven went on hunger strike, one with such unwary thoroughness that he made himself ill. The Welsh regional committee of the National Union of Students deplored the provision of a special one-term course for a single student. Adherents of the Welsh Language Society paraded with posters that inhospitably proclaimed 'No Welcome'. It was as if all the allies of ancient Llewelyn (last native Prince of Wales) were newly risen against an invader.

In Cambridge, too, the Prince had been startled one night

when two young men knocked on his door in New Court, announcing that they were from Aberystwyth and had come to see what he was like. Suspecting a stunt or even a kidnap attempt, Charles had his security drill in mind but quickly realised that the intruders' motives were innocent. Promptly trying out some phrases in Welsh, 'he was rather pleased to find that they were understandable,' one of his visitors reported home. 'An amiable chap with a lively sense of humour – we are all in favour of Charles coming now.'

In May, 1969, the day before the Prince was due, Aberystwyth shopkeepers, however, quietly hid their stocks of joke candles marked 'bomb' and 'dynamite' rather than tempt student enterprise too far. If Prince Charles was a new overdrive to the monarchy, the focus of attention on Wales equally fanned dangerous flames of extremism. Gelignite was found in disused chimneys, hastily dumped machine-guns were retrieved from a lake dredged by the police, a time-bomb blew up at an R.A.F. radio post, and a fanatical plan for an armed uprising ran far beyond the scope of student japes. However, a rapidly spreading joke took the sting from the bomb threats: what time is it by your bomb? Despite these terrors, the royal newcomer found his student hostel on the newer part of the campus, Pantycelyn, reassuringly like a neo-Georgian mansion in the Hampstead Garden Suburb. He was listed as 'Windsor, C., Room 95'; his windows enjoyed a view of Cardigan Bay and his Welsh Nationalist room neighbour companionably took him down to the dining hall the first night.

As it happened, the Prince's Welsh language tutor, Edward Millward, was also Vice President of the Welsh Nationalist party, *Plaid Cymru*, and subsequently Parliamentary candidate for Montgomeryshire. The townsfolk were anxious: undetected militants had attempted to saw the head from the seafront statue of that earlier Prince of Wales, the Duke of Windsor. However, the locals were heartened to find in Charles a young student whose first gesture was to go shopping in the town for coat-hangers, picture hooks and other forgotten necessities. Prince Charles already spoke enough Welsh to get by and had indeed cheerfully tried his phrases on the college cleaners. He was prepared meanwhile to devote five hours a day to the language laboratory, as the College Warden, Mr Ellis, noted with gratification. The Mayor of Llanelly asked Charles on one occasion if he could say Llanelly. 'I said Llanelly,' reported Charles, with wry pleasure, 'and he wiped the saliva out of his eye and said, "Well done".' Despite his busy schedule, Prince Charles also found the time to continue with his Cambridge studies by question-and-answer correspondence with his Trinity history tutor.

Within six weeks, the Prince made his first public speech in Welsh at the League of Youth National Eisteddfod, and thereby wowed an audience of five thousand. His pronunciation was good. He had done his homework. He knew all about a satirical Welsh language recording that was currently in vogue, about 'Carlo' who enjoyed reading one of the amorous Welsh poets in bed. 'I have found time to read Dafydd ap Gwilym in bed,' Charles improved his theme, 'And now I know something about the girls of Llanbadarn.'

More seriously, he spoke of his hope of preserving the Welsh tongue. 'Having spent so many hours in the language laboratory here, I shall certainly never let it die without offering stout resistance.' The tumultuous applause could be heard a mile from the festival marquee, and the Welsh were conquered. 'Charles is the ace in our pack,' said the Mayor of Caernarvon, and Cardiff echoed this sentiment when, wearing military uniform for the first time, Prince Charles accepted the freedom of the city on behalf of his newly-formed Royal Regiment of Wales, 'speaking better Welsh than the Lord Mayor'. And with three weeks to run before the investiture, all Wales recognised that their Prince was a young man of genuine calibre.

II

Like a cloud growing ever-larger on the horizon, the investiture had loomed over Charles for nearly three years. 'Naturally misgivings built up,' he confessed. 'One had an exaggerated picture of the whole situation.' The costuming and cost and the whole apparently obsolete ceremonial aroused nation-wide argument. The ritual had lain defunct for three hundred years until revived with romantic celtic enthusiasm by Lloyd George in 1911. The Prince of Wales at that time, later Duke of Windsor, wrote of being appalled at the fantastic outfit he was expected to wear, 'with its white satin breeches and surcoat of purple velvet'. His mother, Queen Mary, had remonstrated, 'Your friends will understand that as a Prince you are obliged to do certain things that may seem a little silly. It will be only for this once.' Yet in 1969 both the Queen and Prince Philip had felt their qualms of doubt as 'to what extent this sort of virtually medieval revival was relevant'.

For his part, Prince Charles felt he would rather enjoy the dressing-up, the pomp and circumstance. 'As long as I don't get covered too much in egg and tomato I'll be all right.' It was Caernarvon Castle itself that troubled him, not the romantic setting but the implicit difficulties of its use as an amphitheatre for a quasi-religious service mixed with improbable pageantry. 'From the outside you'd wonder why we bother,' he said, 'an open castle, part ruin, with hardly any room, where most of the audience can't see what is going on . . .'

More than a year beforehand when Lord Snowdon visited the Castle with his nephew early one morning, the Prince's imagination was sympathetic and receptive. The two paced from the Water Gate along the intended processional way to the future site of the royal dais and climbed from the Upper Ward to the topmost battlements. Prince Charles had been one of the first to ask the Duke of Norfolk what would happen if it rained, and in his role as Earl Marshal the Duke had merely beamed and said, 'We shall get wet!' But it would not be as simple as that. Stringed instruments cannot be played in a downpour; Charles gave a comic rendering of fanfares reduced to a splutter. As the appointed Constable of Caernarvon Castle, Lord Snowdon was concerned with the modern elements that, all being well, would wed a sense of contemporary history to the celtic and medieval pomp. The royal dais would need a transparent canopy, the orchestras would similarly keep dry beneath acrylic awnings, and pennants and flagstaffs all had to be securely anchored against the strong winds that blow across Caernarvon Bay. Scale models were tested in the wind-tunnels of the Ministry of Aviation. But even so, on the day, some of the banners failed to withstand the winds and hung torn and bedraggled.

As the climax of the proceedings the newly-invested Prince of Wales would be presented to the people from a balcony built within the ancient archway of Queen Eleanor's Gate overlooking Castle Square, the accustomed market-place where the statue of Lloyd George turns a sardonic back on the Castle. But the only alternative, as Charles pointed out, was to turn its back on the people. A more crucial difficulty arose concerning royal transport. With only one major road and one railway into the town, and the royal train taking up one line, the Prince noted, 'I can see all the rest of the special trains backed-up all the way to London.' On practical grounds Charles had to abandon the romantic idea of an arrival by sea with the yacht *Britannia* moored near the Water Gate. Another more personal aspect that 'went the way of all flash' concerned the Prince of Wales' Crown. Made for George II's eldset son, Frederick, in 1729, it is kept among the Crown Jewels in the Tower of London, a diadem of gold, ornamented with gems and pearls from the mines and rivers of Wales, capped with purple velvet and rimmed with ermine. But 'poor Fred, who was alive and is dead' holds no historic renown and, together with the coronet worn by the Duke of Windsor in 1911, the Royal Family regarded this ancient headgear with distaste. At this juncture, one of the oldest guilds of the City of London, the Worshipful Company of Goldsmiths, offered to commission a new coronet of Welsh gold as a gift to the Queen.

If Prince Charles detected goonery in the fact that a local Caernarvon landmark was known as Twt Hill, he also smiled wryly at the swift disclosure that the coronet's appointed designer, Louis Osman, had also once designed a Big Top for Billy Smart's Circus, as well as a concept of an altar cross for Ely Cathedral which had been rejected. After the Queen had approved Mr Osman's first drawings in February, the designer conceded that there was a hint of the crown of thorns in the interweaving fragile shapes of fleurs-de-lys and crosses-patées. But was that not the humblest of all crowns?

Mr Osman also had to bear in mind the need for affinity with the existing investiture regalia designed in 1911 by the Cardiff sculptor, Sir Goscombe John: the ring, formed of two dragons grasping an amethyst; the golden rod or verge of government derived from a shepherd's staff; the sword, with its dragons guarding the crown, the scabbard encircled with the motto *Ich Dien*, I Serve. At one time, indeed, there were two Osman coronets, the first with an unknown and all but undetectable flaw which cracked shortly after the goldsmith's marks were applied. If this imperfect piece had slipped during the ceremony and fallen on the stones of Caernarvon it would probably have shattered into fragments, a terrible omen. So a second coronet – strictly a crown – was made, the seventy-five diamonds and twelve emeralds transferred, the enamelling on platinum renewed, all main elements of this extra task being completed in sixty hours. The new crown weighed only three pounds and Charles wore it around the house for a day or two to get used to it. Great care had been taken that the size, six and seven-eighths, matched his hat size at Lock's; it was a perfect fit.

Yet at the heart of the ritual would be the man, and Prince Charles saw it all – the crown, the gold insignia and mantle – as sacramental, the whole ceremony as meaningful. 'I Serve is a marvellous motto to have,' he said at the time. 'That's the basis of one's job – to serve other people. And a Prince of Wales has to do what he can by influence . . . not by power. There isn't any power, there can be influence . . . in direct ratio to the respect people have for you. I don't want to be a figurehead, but one can reasonably hope to influence people to do what you think is good and useful.'

III

In all the fuss around the investiture, the point was generally overlooked that in deciding to make the event a state occasion, the Queen was taking – in consultation with her Prime Minister, then Mr Wilson – a very considerable decision indeed. In the delicate and unwritten definitions of protocol, the status of a state occasion – involving as it does the supervision and attendance of the hereditary Earl Marshal – is normally reserved for coronations, funerals if so decided, the ceremony of opening Parliament, but little more. Whatever the Duke of Windsor may have subsequently made of it, the 1911 investiture was little more than an extra ceremonial threaded into King George V's coronation year, a Welsh event sandwiched between royal visits to Ireland and Scotland, which the King's official biographer, Harold Nicolson, passes over as 'a local pageant'.

Yet when attending his own first investiture committee, Prince Charles was astonished at the number of people who had come to be involved. The enormous square of baize-draped tables in the Queen Anne room at St James' Palace looked as if they were set for a Commonwealth conference, rather than for planning the programme of a ceremony. The assembly ranged from Lord Lieutenants to an Archdruid – even including a woman Catholic Welsh Archbishop. There were bishops and composers, university professors, lord mayors and police chiefs . . . and the watchful chairman of the Wales Tourist Board. The investiture committee itself proliferated into sub-committees for the religious service, the music, the events, and the preparation of the castle committee in which the name of the Constable of Caernarvon Castle was unhappily listed by the typist as the Earl of Showdon. If Charles seemed crestfallen and subdued that evening, it was because he had never hitherto realised the immense work involved in his own personal and uncomplicated intention of dedication.

Slowly, and ultimately with remarkable efficiency, across a sixteen-month task schedule, the whole operation, dragon-like, lumbered forward. In the early spring of 1969 the lawns of Buckingham Palace blossomed with marking sticks and measuring tapes to represent the steps of the dais and the tele-vision sight-lines, while groups of garden chairs masqueraded as distinguished guests. As the watch-dog of tradition, the then Duke of Norfolk appeared as authoritative on each point of pomp and circumstance as if he had recently discussed the details with Charles I, from whom the few sketchy original precedents derived. 'You're getting quite good at this, Bernard,' the Queen complimented him, after he had compiled one of his infrequent lists of direct questions for her to settle.

Aware that five hundred million would see the ceremony on television or on film, he mentioned to Prince Charles, 'We've got to watch television all the time,' meaning that its needs had to be respected. But when some young B.B.C. men suggested that the dragons might be modernised and simplified for the small screen, the Duke adopted his most reproving expression. 'The heraldic devices are ancient, traditional and correct. There will be no monkeying about.' Nevertheless, the Duke contributed many successful innovations to lessen the tedium of the sixteen processions, having dreamed up some of his best ideas in the bath. Despite a choir of two hundred voices and a score of star singers, the advisory panel of musicians argued that *God Bless the Prince of Wales* should be deleted as it was not up to standard. But the Secretary for Wales, son of a Rhondda miner, made such an impassioned speech in its favour that the anthem was retained and fervently sung 'by all present' at the Prince's first entrance, sweeping the audience with an unforeseen surf of emotion.

Among the debits and credits, the Poet Laureate wrote an investiture poem, although he was not invited to Caernarvon. Some say that the lectern in Welsh slate to hold the Bishop Morgan Bible, the first Bible to be translated into Welsh, was an idea directly suggested by Prince Charles. Others criticised the expense, particularly when the shabbier parts of Caernarvon underwent an extensive repaint. In reality, the paint was offered free by a local paint manufacturing firm.

Many were convinced that the run-up to the investiture was a sophisticated public relations campaign, including as it did the intense enthusiasm engendered by the TV film *Royal Family* and the feature film *A Prince for Wales*, in which Prince Charles was interviewed by David Frost. There was the innovation of a radio interview with the Prince, undertaken by Jack de Manio, and a televised discussion between Charles, Cliff Michelmore and Brian Connell, representing the B.B.C. and independent networks. While it was true enough that David Checketts and Jack de Manio had once worked for the same public relations firm, the whole process of 'putting over Charles' was actually as casual and unprofessional in origin as most royal developments. Brian Connell asked him beforehand how he would react to a question on marriage. 'Well, we'll take it when we come to it,' said Charles unperturbed. And one quotes the sound-track, 'It has got to be somebody pretty special. The one advantage about marrying a princess, or somebody from a royal family, is that they do know what happens. The only trouble is I often feel I would like to marry somebody English or . . .'

'Or Welsh?' interposed Michelmore.

'Or Welsh, or British,' Charles assented, and then agreed, laughing, that he had faltered for a split second. 'I knew that would happen.'

IV

On the eve of the investiture the royal family solved the great transport problem by travelling up in the royal train beforehand and parking for the night in a railway siding outside Bangor, conveniently close to Plas Newydd, the Marquess of Anglesey's home. Some festive evening junketing occurred between house and train, while the surrounding woods and cliffs teemed with troops and policemen in a super-vigilant security alert. Nine bombs and kindred devices had gone off during the months of preparation, not to count the false alarms, hoaxes and foolery: the two sticks of plasticine attached to a ticking alarm clock, for example, which had delayed the royal train for an hour at Crewe. Early on the morning of July 1st, Sir Michael Duff was in his happiest mood as a friend when he greeted the Queen at her railway siding, and on his most scrupulous guard in his role as her Lord Lieutenant of Caernarvonshire. A considerable caval-cade then set out to breakfast at Vaynol, his elegant Queen Anne house, so many royals altogether that the Household travelled by separate jeeps and the Kents crowded blithely into a vegetable van amid the police cars. 'Do you realise,' said the Duke of Beaufort, 'so many royals have never been under one roof before, other than a royal roof?'

'And do you realise,' said Prince Charles, capping him, 'Vaynol has become my home from home?'

Under the stringent security his stroll in the garden that morning required that he should be accompanied by two detec-tives and a bomb expert. When this mild exercise palled, Charles returned to find a re-run of his Michelmore interview on tele-vision. 'It's always me,' he said. 'I'm getting tired of my face.' The Queen was tense and apprehensive for him. After lunch, when the Prince left for the first of the carriage processions from his appointed rendezvous in the Ferodo yard on the outskirts of Caernarvon, an explosion was heard in the distance, mistaken by many for the first boom of a gun salute. Thus heralded, the formalities began; the fanfares sounded, the Prince's personal Welsh banner was broken from the highest turret of the twelfth-century Eagle Tower and, while the audience sang *God Bless the Prince of Wales* with quite unexpected emotion, he was ceremoniously conducted to his octagonal withdrawing-room in the Chamberlain Tower. There he had twenty minutes to wait with David Checketts and his entourage while anxiously watching the arrival of his relatives on television.

The national anthem was the signal for the entry of the Prince of Wales in his own measured procession, preceded by the Wales and Chester heralds of arms, by the Secretary of State for Wales and by Garter King of Arms. There had been a continuous murmur from the onlookers, but now the whole castle was hushed at sight of the youthful and dignified figure, while the cracking of the banners in the wind and the mewing of seagulls seemed only to measure the expectant silence. 'The Prince's only sign of tension was a tendency to clench and unclench his fist upon the hilt of his ceremonial sword', one witness noted.

Prince Charles personally felt that he faced 'an association, a relationship, a title that I want to make as real, productive and effective as possible,' as he had said. Now the dedication was tangible and as he knelt before his mother a few raindrops fell, a soft indeterminate rain, 'warm and gentle as compassion' as another onlooker wrote, rather carried away. In ritual closely based on the Westminster investiture of King Charles I, Prince Charles received from the Queen his ermine mantle in token of leadership, the sword as a symbol of justice, the new-made crown as a token of rank, the ring of Welsh gold in token of duty and the golden verge of pity. Then, to his mother, the Queen, he gave the same pledge of homage given by his father, the strange oath of fealty he had been too young to utter at the Coronation: 'I, Charles, Prince of Wales, do worship, and faith and truth I will bear unto you to live and die against all manner of folks.'

Minutes later he sat on his throne on the Queen's right hand to hear the loyal address from the people of Wales. The difficulty was that he had sat on his own speech and had to wriggle covertly to retrieve it from beneath his robes. The moment of acute embarrassment passed. His reply was in impeccable Welsh, and he added in English, 'I am determined to serve and to try as best as I can to live up to the demands whatever they might be . . .' He had written both his speeches himself, characteristically so when he went on to remind his listeners that Wales had produced 'princes, poets, bards, scholars, and more recently great singers, a very notable goon and several film stars.'

After the religious service, the presentations and processions, the royal family returned to their private transit point at the Ferodo yard. While the Queen went back to London that night, Charles and Anne held a dinner party for the younger set aboard the royal yacht anchored at Holyhead. Percys and Pagets, the Ormsby-Gores, the Nevill cousins, Kerrs and Soames's were there, among other close personal friends, but the party broke up soon after eleven, for the Prince had a duty date early next morning.

He was due at Llandudno as the first appointment of an intensive three-day 'progress through Wales', as the officials dubbed it, three days of meeting as many people as possible, handshake by handshake, attending over forty functions and travelling hundreds of miles by car, jeep, ferry-boat and chopper, returning to sleep aboard *Britannia* each night. 'Eleven p.m. the Prince will leave the Guildhall for the royal yacht . . . ten a.m. (next day) disembark at Swansea . . . via Neath and Aberdare to Merthyr Tydfil,' ran the itinerary. Yet every valley, every city, rang with stories of what the Prince had said and what had happened: how members of the Motorcycle Club of Wales had made up an unofficial escort to ride beside him for twelve miles, how Aberdare had put up a banner – 'Charlie, Aberdare Loves You' – and he had blown kisses in return at a group of pretty girls, how five thousand people packed into the rugby stands at Ebbw Vale had sung *God Bless the Prince of Wales*, and people nearest to him had the impression that his eyes flashed with tears.

The sophisticates admired his competency, the simpler folk were charmed by his readiness and good-natured banter. Among the massive expressions of goodwill, complaints about the cost of the investiture gave way to common agreement that it was worth every penny. The Duke of Norfolk had considered the civil estimates of £200,000 too little. In the event, 4,800 guests purchased their own chairs as souvenirs at twelve pounds apiece, the sale of commemorative medals returned £30,000 to the Royal Mint, and the ultimate cost of £130,000 was set against incalculable touristic advantages. Prince Charles had also demonstrated that he was capable of heading an idealistic new-style establishment, 'equipping the monarchy with overdrive', as one commentator had it.

There was, unfortunately, a tragic sequel to that week in Wales which appalled and sickened the Prince. On the final day of his visit a booby-trap bomb exploded in Caernarvon and gravely injured a young schoolboy playing with a football close by; he had to have a leg amputated. The Prince was about to take a brief respite with Princess Anne in Malta but, extremely distressed and upset, as a close friend testified, he would have preferred to have cancelled his plans and visited the boy's bedside instead, but medical counsel pointed otherwise. His Malta hostess, Lady Dorman, could see how the horrible news had damped his usual spirits. When a fund was raised for the boy, Charles contributed a substantial sum and expressed his sympathy and concern for such 'cowardly and appalling hurt and harm'.

8 Twenty-One and Travel

I

Back at Trinity College for his final year, the Prince of Wales found himself newly installed in a first-floor set of rooms – No. 94 – on the south side of Great Court, where the incessant shuttle of footsteps and the chiming of Wordworth's loquacious chapel clock played counterpoint to the endless plash of Nevile's – or Nevill's – fountain. For a few months more, all history at his elbow, the Prince could sink into the reflective, scholarly atmosphere of Dryden, Byron, Macaulay, Thackeray, Tennyson, Housman, Vaughan Williams and other Trinity men although, in his case, lectures had to compete with royal duties and the more prolonged interruptions of world travel. On the night of November 13th-14th a group of undergraduates clambered to the rooftops to string a banner saying 'Happy Birthday Charlie' opposite his windows. But their bird had flown, by way of an R.A.F. flying lesson, and so to London to spend his twenty-first birthday at the Palace.

His privacy was also to be respected and few people knew that he rose early on his birthday to visit the Chapel Royal of St John in the Tower of London in the company of Princess Anne and the Queen Mother to make 'an act of thanksgiving and dedication for his future life'. After a family lunch, the Prince then celebrated his anniversary in his own way, and pleased those of artistic conscience by holding a concert by Yehudi Menuhin and his newly-formed Festival Orchestra in the Palace ballroom that evening with a programme that included a Mozart violin concerto and his own favourite Haydn cello concerto. Then there were fireworks in the garden, watched by four hundred guests from the balconies and terraces, as if recalling the Buckingham House festivities of George III. 'Most older people, the shoals of ambassadors, left after the fireworks,' one observer noted. 'Then disco and a pop group alternated in the music room, with the picture gallery an acceptable sitting-out room half in darkness. The *Midnight Cowboy* theme. *Everybody's talking at me*, was the most encored. About a hundred and fifty were still dancing at two a.m. and kedgeree was served for breakfast in the Blue Drawing Room at three a.m. . . . The Queen enjoyed the evening with unfettered high spirits, and at one time kicked her shoes off for dancing.

Of the innumerable minor events, the Prince could say, 'It's been a good year.' Earlier on, he had enjoyed a week of skiing in Sweden with his cousin, Crown Prince Carl Gustav, and then there had been the fun of making a television documentary on rural Wales, for which Charles himself had undertaken inter-views with local farmers and other characters. A day or two after his birthday, he relished making a flight to Northern Ireland to become a godfather – 'a refresher course at the font' – at the christening of the Marquis of Hamilton's infant son at the family church in County Tyrone. And so home to Staircase P in Great Court to find a reminder in his new red dispatch box that he would shortly be the richer by £1,278 to close the revenues of his Duchy of Cornwall prime account until the end of the year.

On the other side of the ledger, this sum equated with a necessary expense on his coming-of-age, namely, the cost of the peer's scarlet robe, ermine-collared and decked with four rows of ermine and gold, for the ceremony of his introduction as Prince of Wales to the House of Lords. This occurred on February 11th, 1970, 'played to packed galleries' according to one noble lord. An exceptional number of applications were made for the ballot of seats for peers' wives, and Princess Anne, Princess Margaret and Princess Alexandra formed the nucleus of 'a strong Palace party'. For the first time the Prince's modern crown was borne in state in Parliament, carried upon a crimson velvet cushion. The one awkwardness, as Lord Shackleton realised at the last moment, was that the Prince had no hat to doff on bowing three times to the throne, and a velvet tricorne was hastily borrowed.

The Lords enjoy these inaugurations and, for the Prince, ancient custom had a note of comedy. Sponsored by the Duke of Kent and the Duke of Beaufort, he found that he ironically had to pledge loyalty to himself in repeating the oath at the table. 'I, Charles, Prince of Wales, do swear by Almighty God that I will be faithful and bear true allegiance to Her Majesty Queen Elizabeth, her heirs and successors, so help me God.' In his robes, with his tricorne hat, he felt like a town-crier, he told the Duke of Kent afterwards, cupping his hand to his mouth to cry, 'Oyez, oyez'.

It was four years before his voice was heard in the Lords in his maiden speech on June 13th, 1974, and, by the precedents, this can be considered good going. In the last century, Edward VII, as Prince of Wales, made no attempt to speak until twenty years after his introduction, and then only to voice an innocuous plea for better housing of the poor, citing his own experience as a Sandringham landlord. Neither George V, as Prince of Wales, nor his eldest son when enjoying the same position, seem ever to have addressed the House. Members of the royal family are in any event not expected to engage in controversy, but Prince Charles amusingly told the attendant lords that he had looked up the records for himself and discovered a debate in 1829 when the three royal dukes, Clarence, Sussex and Cumberland, had attacked each other with such uninhibited language that the House was shocked into silence. 'I arrive with some degree of fear and trembling,' the Prince began. 'It is about a hundred years since a member of my family has spoken in this august chamber. But I can assure you I will not create a scene . . .'

The occasion was a debate on the Select Committee on Sport and Recreation. The Prince extolled those who made use of derelict land 'with determination and guts' and praised a Welsh river authority that had remembered the needs of recreation while devising plans for a reservoir ... 'The report must awaken us to the challenge of removing the dead hand of boredom and frustration,' Prince Charles ended his fifteen-minute speech, and had the high satisfaction next morning of finding it reported at half-page length in most of the papers. One columnist discovered with glee that if the Prince had wished he could have claimed £8.50 untaxable expenses and, after all, his sister gained a little pin-money from her riding prizes.

II

There have been few full-scale chronicles of the Duchy of Cornwall. Prince Charles himself felt his sense of comedy wryly touched after he first sat in with his parents at a Duchy council meeting while still in his teens, when the *Court Circular* next day announced that the Duke of Edinburgh and the Prince of Wales had been present, with no mention of his ducal title. To some of us, and to most of the Queen's overseas peoples, the moors and rocky coasts and white clay moonscapes of Cornwall remain as mysterious as the lost lands of King Arthur's Lyonesse. Indeed, the geographic Cornwall, the westward-pointing foreleg of England, from the Devon border towards Land's End and the Scilly Isles, was familiar to its Duke for many years only from the pages of his first atlas.

Historically, Edward, eldest son of Edward III, was created the first Duke of Cornwall by charter in full Parliament at Westminster as a child of only six years, six years also before the King invested him Prince of Wales. Dating from the dispositions of 1066, the estate was largely made up of the possessions of the Earls of Cornwall, the last of whom was King Edward III's brother, and the charter of the year 1337 made it the inheritance of the eldest son of the Sovereign 'for ever'.

Henry V enlarged it, chiefly with ten thousand acres in Somerset; Henry VIII added additional manors in Cornwall, and Charles II bought back lands sold off by Cromwell. When there are no male heirs, the revenues revert to the Crown, and the profits similarly accrue to the eldest son of the Sovereign during his minority. Albert, Prince Consort, handled the Duchy affairs so prudently that he transformed the annual revenue of £16,000 in 1841 into £60,000 on his son's coming-of-age, and the annually invested proceeds had magnificently accumulated to £660,000. Bereft of his father's advice, the then Prince of Wales lavished £220,000 on the purchase of Sandringham. In contrast, Prince Charles came into accumulated capital of £1,270,698,* but nevertheless declined a new car, accepted a polo pony named Tescas which, he said, 'goes like lightning and leaves everyone standing', and in general appeared to think that the financial statistics had little real bearing on his own way of life.

For his twenty-first birthday his Cornish tenantry gave him an eighteenth-century chart of the Scilly Isles; his other gifts ranged from avant-garde cufflinks and a characteristic Venetian painting by Howard Roberts, the Cardiff artist, to a moonscape painting by Lawrence Isherwood and a Welsh Bible. He was delighted to accept a solid silver 'key to the door' from a firm of goldsmiths and some more useful items of gadgetry from family and friends.

Among the donations to the Samuel Beckett theatre in Oxford was a cheque from the Prince; he has always preferred to be a gift-giver rather than a taker, usually in anonymous deeds of generosity. For two or three years the public were none the wiser over the large bottles of whisky sent to every wounded soldier of the Royal Regiment of Wales, as a gesture of sympathy

* Vide the Capital Account of the Duchy of Cornwall for 1970, which disclosed £906,017 in securities, plus £350,582 in recently purchased securities, £13,730 at the Bank of England and £359 at Baring Bros.

from their Colonel-in-Chief. The truth emerged only accidentally when Charles chatted one day with a Ulster veteran who was confined to a wheel-chair, and reporters afterwards enquired what he had said. 'He just asked whether I'd safely received the whisky and he told me it was time I started drinking it.'

More publicly, the Prince of Wales gives half his annual net Duchy revenues to the treasury, 'as a voluntary contribution', the Duchy secretary, Sir Patrick Kingsley, has explained, a gift of more than £100,000 a year to the taxpayer. Since his coming-of-age, this self-divestment has thus cost Prince Charles over half-a-million pounds. By the ancient and hereditary rights of royalty which so enrage Mr William Hamilton, the income and property of the Duchy of Cornwall is exempt from income tax, surtax, capital gains tax and, it appears, the more recent capital transfer tax. With good management year by year, the titular Duke is free of the pangs both of taxation and inflation. He receives no Civil List income, and is accordingly spared the criticism and financial inquiries that repeatedly beset the Queen.

The Duchy today extends far beyond the original geographical boundaries of centuries past when couriers took twelve days to ride on horseback to London. Mixed farms in Devon, Dorset, Gloucester and Wiltshire add to the lucrative total of 129,000 acres yielding a gross £800,000 a year. Although the forest lands are currently barely self-supporting, a more profitable income arises from a gross annual rent-roll of £600,000, with additional rents and royalties from mines and quarries. As a naval joke, Prince Charles loves to utter dire threats about sending miscreants to the Tower or to his own country place, Dartmoor Prison, on which he receives a ground rent from the Prison Commissioners. Duchy management expenses total £657,000 per annum, and there are medieval side-strings that may well mystify anyone except Mr Parker, the Duchy auditor.

The enigmatic Office of Havenor – derived from haven or shelter – thrives on the proceeds of the sale of unclaimed wrecks.

An annuity in lieu of tin coinage duties and tolls and post groats, whatever they may be, still yields £16,000 a year. In the heart of London, the forty-five Duchy acres in Kennington, south of the river, are the last residue of a rural retreat and hunting-ground of the Black Prince, an asset annually bringing in £300,000 from commercial and housing property. As light relief after inspecting a housing scheme, Prince Charles strolled into a pub there one morning, cheerfully claiming it as *his* local. There are of course many other pubs and perquisites in the west country. If an intestate dies without heirs in the Duchy, the Duke of Cornwall ultimately gets the cash. The same is true of treasure trove, and the Duke is similarly entitled to royal fish, which is useful if a sturgeon should yield Cornish caviar but a costly nuisance when the stranded carcase of a whale has to be cleared away as a ducal responsibility.

Prince Charles is well informed on such details. Making an unofficial reconnaissance of the west country in April, 1969, he knew that Cornish granite had helped repair Chelsea Bridge and knew, too, that his granite chippings still served to repair roads as far away as Yorkshire. 'He sees all the papers of the Duchy,' says Earl Waldegrave, acting managing director of Duchy affairs (who thrives also as Lord Warden of the Stannaries, a prestige derived from the Latin *stannum* – tin). 'Like any other estate owner, he comes to the meetings; we are in constant touch with him. He can see graphs, what is happening to the rents, things of that sort.'

A minor item of the annual Accounts refers to the entertainment of Duchy tenants on rent days, 'audit dinners', as they are known. In the Dorset manor of Fordington, villagers roast a sheep on the village green every St George's Day and supposedly send a leg of mutton to Prince Charles wherever he may be. When the Prince first *officially* toured the Duchy, just after his twenty-fifth birthday, he found himself involved in a charade of feudal dues. The mayor of Launceston presented him with a pound of pepper, another official knelt to offer a pound of herbs, a forester came to Launceston green with a load of firewood as a rent in kind, and Charles, pre-occupied just then with naval service, looked suitably startled on next being brought a pair of white greyhounds. The Prince wished his tenants 'peaceable and quiet seizin', while officials looked agitated when he seemed about to do some quiet seizing himself and his dues – a hunting bow, a salmon spear, gauntlets, grey cloak and the greyhounds complete – were about to be put in his car. But the regal jester was only having his fun. Borrowed for the occasion, the greyhounds were returned to their owner next day and for the most part, the feudal dues returned to their display cases in the Launceston Museum.

The proportion of cash that the Prince returns to the Treasury is subject to review on his marriage. And by those contingencies that needs must be considered in advance, the 1971 Select Committee on the Civil List proposed £60,000 a year for the Princess of Wales as his widow.

III

Happily, life is not all landmarks and watersheds. Having attained his majority, Prince Charles returned to his history studies, aware that intensive work and play alike would be crammed into the year ahead. Following a fashionable Cambridge craze, he also launched into an eight-week course of 'rapid reading', which might be described as the useful art of skimming, taking in a page top to bottom rather than reading line by line. In the Spring term, with the exams 'looming behind barricades of overseas travel', he had all too little time to spare for his commitments to a second Dryden Society revue, *Quiet Flows the Don*.

The title alluded to academics rather than Russian novels. Charles said modestly that he was in at least four of the sketches, but at the Sunday night private preview the gentlemen of the press discovered that, more accurately, he played in all but five of the thirty scenes. He had borrowed a tweed cap for a *Peyton Place* satire, he rolled on the floor battling with bagpipes as a television antiques expert, he was a deep-sea sports commentator, he blew bubbles as a B.B.C. weather forecaster ... and as a penalty of undertaking too much he forgot his lines.

The girl in the prompt corner had no script. 'This doesn't happen on the B.B.C.,' the Prince ad-libbed. But then he recovered. 'Wales will blow. Guernsey and Jersey will be warm and lovable with a high milk yield ...' While Richard Burton was appearing in London in a film as King Henry VIII, the presumed future King Charles III appeared nightly in Cambridge for a week's run. The Queen and Princess Anne were in the audience one evening, having dined with Charles in his panelled rooms in Great Court beforehand, savouring the Tudor atmosphere and the novelty. The Queen had hitherto twice lunched with her son in his former lair in New Court, but in this new and dignified setting she had cause to divine the firm and serious individuality rapidly maturing behind his flow of fun and badinage.

There is always a risk that parents consider their offspring young for their age. In that same February of 1970, Prince Philip whisked Charles off to Strasbourg to attend a conservation conference under the auspices of the Council of Europe, initiating his son into a sphere of wider international statesmanship after his previous conference experience gained in Wales and London. As so often, the weekend provided Philip with an opportunity to visit his sisters, Margarita and Sophie, one of those 'other family' occasions which Charles knew his father adored. But this time a note of sadness infused the reunion, for Prince Philip's mother, Charles' Mountbatten grandmother, Princess Alice of Greece, had died at Buckingham Palace shortly before Christmas, not two months after the death of her second daughter, Princess Theodora of Baden, Prince Charles' 'Aunt Dolla'.

In an atmosphere of family conference, Charles and his cousins made a close-knit younger social group of their own: Prince

Guelf and Prince George of Hanover, who had been at Gordonstoun; their younger sister, Princess Frederica, who was then fifteen, and their elder half-sister, Princess Clarissa of Hesse. Though only a year or two older than Charles, Guelf was already married, having made a match that ignored courtly and ancient precedents. Clarissa, too, though three years older than Charles, used to blush prettily during visits to Windsor at seeing her name in the *Court Circular*, as if someone had deemed it prudent to signpost a potential Victoria and Albert relationship of first cousins. But such fond match-making prospects now left the cousins quite undisturbed, and Princess Clarissa married a Frenchman named Claude-Jean Derrien the following year and repeated quite a different family pattern, that of her grandmother, by setting up house near Paris.

'I've never specified whom he should marry,' Philip remarked of Charles, around this time. 'People tend to marry within their own circles. The advantage, perhaps, is a certain built-in acceptance of the sort of life you are going to lead.' Inevitably, the world's more ebullient newspapers and popular magazines embarked on their fruitless quest of guessing the girl.

'It's disreputable,' said Prince Charles of some of the wilder foreign stories, 'but everybody reads them. I suppose I must accept that what happens to me can be newsworthy regardless.' Guelf could commiserate from practical experience; he and his pretty Wibeke von Gunsteven had come under similar surmise in the German weeklies. Charles understood that the incessant quiz had been worse for his mother in the late 1940s and much worse for his Aunt Margo in the 1950s. There were a few photogenic debs, whom reporters and cameramen readily recognised, who could be singled out in the royal group at a theatre though perhaps the girl was partnering one of Charles' friends and he had hardly spoken to her. When that happened, and he read the gossip next day, he used to ring her up and apologise, 'in the most charming way, you know, making fun but not too much fun'.

The contrast of rumour and reality was instanced by the gifted and beautiful Miss Lucia Santa Cruz, elder daughter of the then Chilean ambassador to London, whom Charles first met at Cambridge when she was helping Lord Butler with his memoirs, particularly the historical research to check his account of the Munich period. The Prince, as it happened, was preparing a paper on the same era. Older than Charles by three years, she sat opposite him at dinner one night and mentioned her plans to write a book on the reign of Charles IV. 'Really?' the Prince said, playing up. 'Who on earth was he?' Lucia teasingly identified him as the second son of Charles III. 'That's right,' said Charles, on course all the while. 'Weren't both kings of Spain when we had George the Third?'

On the recall of her father to Santiago after a Marxist coup, Lucia returned home, only to reappear in London two years later and to be immediately invited to Balmoral, as might a courier with news. One could not help smiling at the headlines that the Prince of Wales was at Balmoral with a mystery blonde and that both travelled – sinful shades of the Orient Express – 'on the overnight train'. No mention that they were both respectably at the Castle with the Queen and her guests, the King and Queen of Tonga.

'I have absolutely no idea what my image is,' the Prince once told a group of magazine editors. 'I therefore intend to go on being myself to the best of my ability,' and in general the press treated him sympathetically. Some elements may have longed for a new-style Nellie Clifden scandal, the young actress smuggled into 'Bertie's' (Edward VII's) quarters at the Curragh, or a 'bride of Malta', or even a Julie Stonor, the attractive Roman Catholic with whom Prince Charles' great-grandfather, George V, underwent a romantic and hopeless youthful love affair. But Bertie was still in his teens at the time of the Curragh affair and 'Georgie' not yet twenty-one when his mother praised him for having 'resisted all temptation so far'. Bertie at nineteen had already undertaken a solo tour in the United States and Canada, with such popular success that at one of his final engagements in New York the ballroom floor collapsed under the sheer weight of those crowding to see him. At fifteen, Georgie had sailed before the mast in H.M.S. *Bacchante*, in company with his elder brother, the Duke of Clarence, and a senior midshipman whose 'almost feminine ways and silly over-deference induced them to take liberties with him which they should not,' as their tutor, Mr Dalton, scrupulously reported.

Some were surprised that at Cambridge Prince Charles remained aloof from his own permissive generation. 'He's got a very easy social manner with girls,' Lord Butler noted. He was sociable, affectionate and demonstrative with those of the opposite sex whom he knew well, but also unfailingly considerate and chivalrous, 'as if he knows the drill about knights in shining armour *sans reproche*. Or perhaps in his case a white knight complete with Lewis Carroll clowning,' as one of his contemporaries wrote with insight.

The Prince remained uninvolved, as if he had attached himself to a computerised calendar, whirring and planning far into the future. The girls with whom he danced, whom he squired to theatres, with whose parents he enjoyed weekend hospitality, and the majority of the young ladies photographed and named in the newspapers are now happily married.

Meanwhile, in 1970, Prince Charles was more exclusively preoccupied with the pattern of events immediately ahead, the widening horizons of travel, and the experience one might expect from training with the armed Services, 'the traditional thing to do and also, I think, a very sensible thing. A period in the Service gives you great experience and responsibility, of life, of discipline and above all of people.'

He would happily elaborate on this theme in a television interview, but when the topic of marriage was raised during preliminary discussion in the studio, he merely responded, think it's much too soon to talk about that.'

IV

The last months at Cambridge were not without ennui. When the Prince of Wales joined his parents and Princess Anne on the royal tour of New Zealand and Australia in 1970, one acquaintance felt that 'he leapt on the band-wagon as though his life depended on it.' Flying out in early March, he was 'in elated mood' at Wellington on greeting Anne and his parents who had sailed aboard the *Britannia* from Tonga. This royal visit, the first for seven years, saw the first try-out of the walkabout technique, originally an idea of his sister's, in which Charles joined enthusiastically, 'like being at some enormous party', as they told their first weekend hosts, the Aclands, at their high-country sheep station. The weather produced a New Zealand autumn at its wettest, but neither downpours nor puddles could quench Charles' enthusiasm, dancing country-style at a Y.M.C.A. reception, squelching through the mud to a stadium pop concert and revelling in a weekend of fishing between showers.

When some Otago university students shouted 'Queen, go home!' Charles said, 'Well, that's a bit rough,' and added that he had hopes of living down a monarchy-versus-republic opinion poll in Australia the previous month which elicited a sixty-five per cent vote for 'King Charles now'. This was royal repartee in new coinage, 'having fun with the folks', as Charles described it. The royal visit to Australia was particularly to commemorate the bicentenary of Captain Cook's first landing and Charles freshly scored popularity points in Sydney when he said that, personally, he felt he was celebrating his homecoming.

Yet this was no more than true. 'He talks of feeling at home all the time,' Prince Philip told the New South Wales premier, Robin Askin. At Government House, Canberra, on Easter Monday, father and son found themselves trying out polo ponies, and Charles remarked, 'It's incredible! I can't believe we're over ten thousand miles from Windsor.' He tried out things he had not got around to before, surf-riding at Bondi Beach and the quieter Coogee Beach, where two onlookers tried to take a rise out of him by asking if he spoke Greek. 'Yes, I can say "Push off",' said Charles, but more strongly, and this story, too, added marks to his score.

'You're my favourite bloke,' said a blushing young nun in Tasmania. 'That's very nice,' Charles thanked her, looking as if he really meant it. From Melbourne he took Princess Anne to see Timbertop. 'That school's probably the reason why, whenever I come back to Australia, I experience a curious and inexplicable sensation that I belong,' he told a rally of young farmers with conviction. A little of the fizz noticeably went out of the royal tour on April 8th when he broke away to return to his studies at Cambridge. But he had also been invited to make a five-day stopover in Japan, and here again he later summed up the experience as 'terrific'.

If the Prince had tried to be Aussie in Australia, he now attempted not to appear too outlandish in Japan. The brief visit had been widely publicised as his first mission on his own, which is royal language for a suite of six and a welcoming press reception of several hundred. 'I really think they should have an asylum waiting for one at the end of these long flights,' he said in an aside to Frank Robertson of the *Telegraph*. 'One's metabolism definitely goes haywire.' Yet others did not suspect his fatigue, and his hectic welcome was merely the overture. After a British Embassy reception, he dined with the Emperor Hirohito – forging one of the many links of statecraft that culminated in the Queen and Prince Philip's 1975 state visit to Japan – and was ready next day for an early start on the famous 150 m.p.h. 'bullet train' to Kyoto, and a round of temples, castles and palaces in the ancient Imperial capital.

Sir John Pilcher, the British Ambassador, wondered where he found the stamina. In the annex of the Miyako Hotel, Charles elected to live Japanese style, sleeping on a straw pallet on the floor and bathing in a scented cedar tub. He showed exceptional dexterity with chopsticks and, stiff-backed after sitting for two hours on a straw mat in a restaurant, he accepted a geisha's offer to massage his back, thanking her in Japanese, 'Arigato! Arigato!' when he assumed his jacket. He had done his homework. The abbot who showed him around the temple of the great bronze Buddha was equally impressed by his intelligent questions on Shinto philosophy. 'I found that what the old man was saying I had believed, without realising it, all my life,' Prince Charles said afterwards, encouraging words from the future head of the Church of England and not inexplicable to a younger generation who seek the common truths of religion rather than the differences.

Yet in winning the friendship of Japan, the Prince, 'charming, easy-going, tactful', excelled himself in his marathon stint at the international Expo '70, where he toured twenty-one pavilions and then made the imaginative gesture of giving a party for the seventy-seven nations and others represented, requesting that each should send two under-thirty members of their staff. Meeting the President of the Sony company, Mr Akio Morita, he heard of the plans to build a Sony plant in Europe. 'Why not in Wales?' the Prince suggested and promptly outlined a few of the advantages, with the happy sequel that four years later the Prince opened a new Sony factory in Glamorgan.

V

Within a month of returning home, Prince Charles sat his History Tripos exams along with 204 other students; the ordeal was to last a week. Telephoning the Queen on her forty-fourth birthday, when she was cruising in the royal yacht off the Great Barrier Reef, he sounded in good spirits. Perspiring in the venerable atmosphere of Old Schools, working on the six papers, each of three hours, he felt himself confident in assessing Hitler's seizure of power, quaking in doubt at the seventeenth-century expansion of Europe, probably okay on Winston Churchill as 'an unsuccessful peacetime Minister', and reassurred in turn on Louis XIV as 'king of the vile bourgeoisie'. With their valid historical interest, the Prince's papers rest today in the royal archives, but one should explain that the examiners first assessed and marked the papers and only later looked up the names of the students. For all the interruptions of his career, 'Wales, H.R.H. Prince of' gained his Bachelor of Arts degree in Class 2, Division 2, which was a good average triumph. And so, with the first honours degree – as distinct from honorary degree – ever gained by an heir to the Throne, Prince Charles was comparatively free and unfettered for some months to come.

He had been unhappy at missing Tonga on the royal tour, and within a week or two of the exam results one knew that the Queen had promised him Fiji instead, where he was to represent her during the Independence celebrations. But first he latched on to the Queen and Prince Philip's tour through the Canadian Arctic that July, paying a visit on his own to the Micheners at Government House, Ottawa; 'wonderfully diplomatic, attentive, gregarious', as an aide to the Governor-General reported to me. To cap this ambassadorial interlude, Charles asked Premier Trudeau's niece, Jocelyne Rouleau, whether she would like to come along on the Arctic trip 'for the fun', with the result that Pierre Trudeau and Mlle Rouleau flew into Frobisher Bay airport twelve minutes before the Queen's plane.

Jocelyne was also twenty-one and for a few days, with Princess Anne, they formed a carefree trio while the Queen and Prince Philip were occupied with their own fuller schedule. Gazing from the window of his new-built hotel, Charles had been delighted at the 'jungle of ice blocks' in the bay. It was fun to fish for cod Eskimo-style through the ice close inshore, fun to fish for his breakfast at midnight in a nearby fresh-water river, landing six trout-like Arctic graylings, fun to join a hamburger barbecue and, not least, to wait up for the midnight sun into the small hours to find that he had been correct in forecasting that 'no performance tonight' could occur through the rain clouds. Despite the ravenous mosquitoes and black-fly he felt, as his father had done, the extraordinary spell of the northland solitudes. Later, in Manitoba, he captured the characteristic Canadian sense of gusto, making a canoe jaunt along the Red River, visiting a prairie horse show at Swan River and taking a helicopter swirl along the shores of Duck Bay. Then brother and sister continued their journey with what Charles called 'a sensational climax' when he and Anne parted from their parents in Winnipeg to fly south to Washington with the Nixon sisters, Tricia and Julie, and Julie's husband, David Eisenhower.

Knowing nothing of the dire scandals ahead for the Nixons, the five young people could not have been happier, all so nearly the same age. Nor did the supposed private nature of Charles' and Anne's visit to the States prevent fanfares, both of herald trumpeters on the lawns of the White House and headlines in huge type in the American press. Charles was the first Prince of Wales to sleep in the White House since Albert Edward in 1860, and, like his predeccessor, he cruised down the Potomac to Mount Vernon. 'Bertie' had found George Washington's 'much revered homestead falling into decay', and Charles found it difficult to judge its charm amid the wild scrimmage in the small rooms of commentators and cameramen. When Bertie had visited the opera in America, the audience had spontaneously sung *God Save the Queen*. When Charles and Anne paid an impromptu visit to an open-air concert in Lafayette Park, the audience rose similarly in a storm of applause while the orchestra broke into Elgar's march, *Pomp and Circumstance*. For more modern overtones amid the helicopter flips, the barbecues and dances, the Prince found the first men on the moon, Neil Armstrong and Frank Bormann, waiting to greet him at the Smithsonian Institute. 'This is wonderful!' he told Neil Armstrong. 'I've been jealous of my two young brothers ever since they met you back home last year.'

There were some who felt that Prince Charles had adopted a

'wonderfully controlled naïvety' as an asset to his public charisma. He was a seasoned voyager when late that autumn he made a half-hour speech to five thousand members of the Institute of Directors at the Albert Hall and so addressed the biggest audience he had faced in his career to date. 'Whoever invited me exploited my extreme innocence. I assumed you were a small business organisation. Little did I know I had agreed to speak to five thousand whizz kids, tycoons, industrial giants . . .' And he elaborated that a twenty-minute talk with President Nixon in his office in the White House had lasted 'to my amazed embarrassment an hour and a half'. In Fiji, where he had seen the Union Jack hauled down, the newly independent nation had immediately joined the Commonwealth. 'She must believe there is some value in it.' In Bermuda an opposition party had boycotted him as 'representing the forces of imperialism . . . But the Commonwealth is a group of nations of mutual understanding concerning freedom and democracy. That by any standards is a jolly good start.'

The sustained applause would have been remarkable for any speaker and this was an audience of professionals. As a stylist, 'pretending naïve ignorance and then speaking forcefully for his own generation' he had entoiled them all in his web of personal experiences and impromptu asides, 'like listening to one's own son', according to one warm analysis.

9   The Services

Prince Charles celebrated his twenty-second birthday with a second concert at Buckingham Palace, naturally not so splendid an occasion as for his twenty-first, although one remembers an unusual cello piece with accompaniment by the Welsh harpist, Osian Ellis. That weekend the Marquess and Marchioness of Salisbury entertained the Prince at Hatfield House, and the inquisitive or eager who sought for a suitable young lady in the family could find only a grand-daughter then aged fifteen, Rose Gascoyne-Cecil.

To add to the difficulties of my more distant readers who would wish to understand every complex facet of English social life, Salisbury is the denoting title of the Cecil famiy, just as Abergavenny is the chief distinction of the Nevills and the ducal title of Devonshire is that of the Cavendish line. The Cecils have featured in the patterns of royal friendships since the Tudors, with a renewal of political power in Victorian times when the third Marquess of Salisbury became Prime Minister. Talking to Prince Charles that anniversary weekend, his elderly host, the fifth Marquess, must have keenly perceived his heightened inner strength and confidence, as if the political storm-clouds in Bermuda, his rapturous reception on an accompanying visit to Barbados, his State duties in Fiji and the naïve ceremonies of homage in the Gilbert and Ellice Islands had all enhanced his stature unaware.

Certainly this happy, modest, personable young man was no longer the boy who, at Vaynol not two years earlier, had turned crimson when Sir Michael Duff had chanced to ask, 'Would you like something to drink, sir?' Misinterpreting his blush, Duff had added, 'Or aren't you allowed to drink, or something?' and Charles had awkwardly answered, 'No, it's not that – it's just that I'm not used to being called Sir!' But with all the assurance in the world, in his public persona, he had beamed at the assembled politicians in Bermuda (celebrating their 350th year of Parliament) and said to them, 'Bearing in mind that I am the first Charles to have anything to do with a Parliament for 320 years, I might have turned nasty and dissolved you!'

Now the recognition of his major role in national and commonwealth affairs came from every quarter. As *Punch* put it, he had emerged 'in his own right', and the journal supplied one of the minor embellishments of English custom by inviting him to the weekly editorial lunch, where he obliged tradition by carving his initial on the hallowed editorial table and learned in return that there were fifty-two pubs in London bearing the name of the Prince of Wales and only nine enhanced by the presumed future distinction of his wife.

In March, 1971, Prince Charles was offered the Freedom of the City of London, and the boy who had once watched the soldiers from the garden wall of Clarence House, the boy grown to manhood, drove in an open landau with his sister from Buckingham Palace to the Guildhall through dense waiting crowds who cheered and applauded him every yard of the way. Only a few days earlier he had gained another adult acknowledgement by being lunched at No. 10 by the Prime Minister, Mr Heath, and now the top Establishment of the City of London and its guests, 'the elect seven hundred', rose to give him an immense ovation.

I felt at the time that he had never seemed more dignified and handsome, wearing his ceremonial uniform as Colonel-in-Chief of the Royal Regiment of Wales, with the riband and star of the Order of the Garter. Yet it was still a youngster who sat, grinning broadly with immense amusement, as the declaration of patrimony was read out, according to the centuries-old ritual, asserting that he was the son of 'the Prince Philip, Duke of Edinburgh, Citizen and Fishmonger of London, and that he was born in lawful wedlock . . . his son so reputed and taken to be, and so they all say.'

He was still sun-tanned from a two-week camera and fishing safari in Kenya that had made one of the last unfulfilled dreams of his boyhood come true. He had flown out with Princess Anne, who would herself soon be twenty-one and was undertaking her *Blue Peter* film project for the Save the Children Fund. By coincidence it was just nineteen years to the day since their mother had been staying up-country at the Treetops lodge on the morning of destiny when she became Queen. Princess Anne planned to spend a night at the hotel on the site, but Charles did not wish to get in the way of the film unit and evidently felt it pointless to pilgrimage to the spot when the original wild fig tree and the look-out post in its branches had long since been burned down. Instead, he had hurried on with David Checketts by air, bus and motorboat direct to the remote Ferguson's Gulf fishing lodge on Lake Rudolf, from which he had then walked for fifty miles on a four-day trek with pack-camels through the Ngare Ndare game reserve.

The British High Commission aide, Frank Steele, called the journey 'hilarious . . . I've never laughed so much in all my life.' The Prince's own favourite safari story was of being awakened at night by the noise of the camels panicking and, clear in the moonlight, thirty paces from his sleeping bag, was a rhinoceros. 'I was completely in the bag, but he snorted and walked away.' In Nairobi, before rejoining Anne, he also held with the Queen's special authority a brief investiture, knighting the President of the East Africa Court of Appeal, now Sir William Duffus, and decorating others with the C.B.E. and O.B.E. This was his first bestowal of knighthood in his life, if not a taste of kingship, giving the accolade in quiet solemnity with two quick touches of his Royal Regiment sword.

Now, in the Guildhall, he again looked an inch taller as he

replied to the presentation of the freedom scroll by the City
Chamberlain, who, by the happiest auspices, was a Mr
Richard Whittington. It had been announced some months
earlier that the Prince of Wales would follow royal tradition by
joining the Royal Navy after taking an advanced flying course
with the Royal Air Force, and the occasion enabled him to refer
to a critical minority in a speech very obviously in his own
words.

'It is pointless and ill-informed to say that I am entering a
profession trained in killing ... The Services in the first place
are there for fast, efficient and well-trained action in defence.
Surely the Services must attract a large number of duty-
conscious people? Otherwise who else would subject themselves
to being square-bashed, shouted at by petty officers, and made
to do ghastly things in force ten gales? I am entering the R.A.F.
and then the Navy because I believe I can contribute something
to this country by so doing. To me it is a worthwhile occupation
and one which I am convinced will stand me in stead for the
rest of my life.'

On the following Monday he presented himself for duty at
the R.A.F. College, Cranwell, little realising that he was em-
barking on one of his great absorptions of the next five years.

II

Cranwell is often said to be in the wind-swept wilds of Lincoln-
shire. It lies, in fact, midway between the cathedral city of
Lincoln and the market centre of Grantham (home town of Mrs
Margaret Thatcher), a conurbation of six square miles of air-
fields and parade grounds, enormous engineering blocks, streets
of houses for four thousand people, and college buildings that
would not dismay Sir John Betjeman. On March 8th, 1971, the
Prince of Wales began his journey from Windsor into the Royal
Air Force by helicopter, an auspicious choice as it seemed later,

The Prince of Wales wearing his
robes as Knight of the Order of the Garter.
(*Camera Press*)

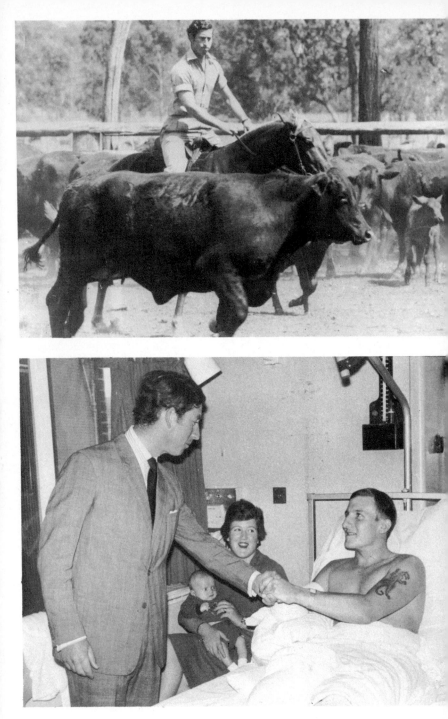

Above: On a cattle station in Queensland, 1974.
(*Keystone Press Agency*)
Below: The Prince and the bomb victim: encouragement for Corpo
Paul Thomas of the Welsh Guards, 1975.
(*Press Association*)

he godfather: Prince Charles with the infant son of the Duke and Duchess of Gloucester, February, 1975.
(*Camera Press*)

Cousin Charles: an impromptu reel with
Lady Sarah Armstrong-Jones at Balmoral.
(*Camera Press*)

An investiture in Nairobi, 1971.
(*Keystone Press Agency*)

Above: A private study in contentment:
the royal angler casts his line.
(*Camera Press*)

Below: 'A most horrifying expedition!'
The Prince during a commando assault course.
(*Press Association*)

After an Arctic dive at Resolute Bay,
the Prince demonstrates the fun of inflation.
(*The Associated Press*)

Above: Prince Charles at the controls of
a Wessex 5 Commando helicopter, 1975.
(Camera Press)

Below: Taking his first command in the Royal Navy,
The Prince is piped aboard *H.M.S. Bronington*, 1976.
(Keystone Press Agency)

and at the R.A.F. Benson airfield he transferred to the twin-engined Bassett on which by then he had already logged sufficient extra flying hours to merit the rank of Flight Lieutenant.

Fortunately, also, for those – not least himself – who wished the Prince to have nothing the easy way, the new system of Graduate Entry eased the officer training course. Under the old system, cadet training had occupied two and a half years. Under the new, a degree course at university ranked as the time element of academic training and necessitated a flying course of only another year before the cadet could receive his R.A.F. wings. For Prince Charles, individual tuition was in fact to be compressed into five months in order that he could then enter Dartmouth Royal Naval College. Unlike his Windsor grandfather, George VI, who between Cranwell and the Air Ministry had felt like a memo marked 'Passed to you for action, please', every phase of his jet-flying course was decisively clearcut, provided that he satisfactorily passed each successive requirement.

The first was that he should fly a 480 miles per hour training jet on the third Monday after arrival, on completion of an intensive ground school course. Seventeen years earlier, when Philip wanted to learn to fly jets, a public outcry had centred upon the question of how far the 'irreplaceable leaders of a nation' could be justified in taking avoidable risks. But time had flown on and now controversy centred only upon whether the two training aircraft used by the heir to the throne should be more rigorously tested and serviced than others. Prince Charles' sympathies lay with the public view that they should not. He found it a cause of personal irritation that his tuition should be known by the operational code name Golden Eagle. He would have preferred a less flamboyant symbol, and his ears reddened like signal lamps when the Station Commandant spoke of Cranwell's pride at training 'a precious piece of the nation's property'.

At a more sensible level, the Prince was given quarters resembling a two-floored maisonette in the western wing of the

5—PC * *

main college building which he would occupy with three other
officer cadets of his own age. His bedroom and sitting-room
were on the first floor, where he shared a bathroom with an
alert and dapper neighbour from Wolverhampton, Flying Officer
Jim Giles, while the other two cadets and the Prince's detective
were housed on the floor below.

All five shared the same batman. Prince Charles breakfasted
in his own room – cornflakes and honey, a glass of milk, no tea
or coffee, the proved time-saving recipe—before he got through
a quick processing of newspapers and correspondence in time
for the met. briefing at eight a.m. The second week saw a photo
session at the swimming-bath building after dinghy drill, inflat-
ing his Mae West and dinghy for the benefit of the cameras –
and R.A.F. public relations material – after diving off the ten-
metre board. Landing drill next in the gymnasium, how to break
the impact when landing with the velocity of a parachute jump.
No lectures that morning but worksheets to be answered:
twenty highly technical questions on aircraft problems. Lunch at
the aircrew buffet, cafeteria style, then 'ejector seat indigestion',
learning the know-how of being hurled into space, followed by
more aircraft drill and more work-sheets for homework. It was
small wonder that Flight Lieutenant, the Prince of Wales, unlike
Charles the undergraduate, had no time to take part in the
annual Cranwell revue.

Like everyone else on the station, he moved around fast on
a R.A.F.-issue bicycle, but for more distant destinations he had
indulged himself on his birthday with an Aston Martin DB6
Volante, dark blue, complete with stereo, one of the fastest cars
on the road. Minutes only then to Belvoir Castle, where the
Duke and Duchess of Rutland invited him to a charity ball and
all the gossips said that Charles and the Duke's daughter,
Charlotte, made a charming swinging couple. It was little more
than an hour also to Wood Farm, where the Prince was punc-
tilious in returning hospitality. But it was on March 29th, a day
or two before his Belvoir Castle visit, that he logged his first Jet

Provost flight on schedule, and then he flew solo in the following month. Within three months he had clocked some eighty hours flying time with the Provosts, twenty-four of them solo.

In later private correspondence, the Prince handsomely gave credit to Dick Johns, who had begun working with him at the Bassett training stage and was his personal supervisor through Cranwell. Squadron Leader Johns was in his early thirties, young enough to withstand his pupil's larky side. On April 1st he remained unconvinced, for instance, when a special announcement over the Tannoy expressed the regret of a London firm of shoemakers that a fault had been found in the design of shoes bought by cadets and asked any such purchasers to hand in their shoes at the porter's lodge for modification. Several dozen pairs, it is said, were handed in by April fools before the royal prank was tumbled.

Straight-faced, Charles pretended at times to be comically muddled, riding out to the wicket on a horse during a charity cricket match, carrying a polo stick. After that journal of good grooming, the *Tailor and Cutter*, had criticised his 'cult of shabbiness' he arrived at an immaculate Master Tailors' dinner wearing an old hacking jacket over his white waistcoat and Order of the Garter, and solemnly seemed none the wiser until after grace when, amid laughter, he removed the coat to disclose resplendent evening dress. Some miles from Cranwell, he turned up with his flat-mates one evening to drink bitter and play darts at the Britannia Inn, 'confusing you with a yacht of the same name'.

Off duty on Wednesday afternoons, the Prince made other explorations, buying National Trust tickets unrecognised at Tattershall Castle and, another time, climbing the 364 steps of Boston Stump for its immense view over the Wash, enjoying probably his only chance of ever being an unimpeded tourist in his own country. No one looks twice at an airman in Lincoln and he was undisturbed in exploring the glories of the cathedral. Among the crowds in Newark market, however, he was detected and had to make his escape in his Aston Martin, after smiles and handshakes all round.

Meanwhile, his jet-flying course continued with 'familiarisation' in R.A.F. front-line aircraft. He made operational sorties over the North Sea in a Nimrod maritime reconnaissance jet from the Strike Command base at Leuchars and gained a favourable report flying as co-pilot in a supersonic Phantom jet fighter which, could he have forsaken discipline, would have carried him to New York in five hours. And inhabitants of Doncaster may care to know that in June, 1971, they underwent a high-level bombing attack by the Prince of Wales during a simulated three-hour sortie with a Vulcan bomber, in which the railway yards and locomotive works all suffered 'direct' hits.

In July, hearing via the grapevine that he would get his wings, the Prince noted his intense pleasure at becoming 'as near a professional as I can ever hope to be on Jet Provosts'. To his parents and to certain air chiefs, however, he mentioned with less satisfaction that unlike other cadets he hadn't yet had a go at parachuting. 'Well,' said the Queen drily – so the story goes – 'I certainly cannot stand in your way.'

The available records were reticent on whether any other member of the royal family had ever actually made a parachute jump. Certainly no one so close in the Succession. The one heart-in-mouth air hazard for Charles had been the previous year in the Bassett over Sussex when a Piper Aztec had suddenly appeared ahead, an estimated three seconds from collision point. Prince Charles for a change was piloting his father, with an instructor also in the plane but the 'air miss' discomfited the personnel concerned with traffic control.

Considerable caution, then, surrounded Prince Charles' parachute jump, to be taken from an altitude of 1,200 feet, into the sea a mile out from Poole on a summer day in perfect weather. First of all, remindful drill and emergency procedure at the Parachute Training school at Abingdon. For company, three other cadets in the Andover transport who were to jump in turn.

First, a Command Parachute Officer was to jump and 'drift' to prove the direction of the wind, and next out was the officer in charge of Abingdon. But the Prince has given us his own account. 'Out I went ... the slipstream is terrific. You appear to be flipped on your back and the next thing I knew my feet were above my head caught in the rigging lines, very odd. I thought, "They didn't tell me anything about this." Fortunately my feet weren't twisted round the lines and came out very quickly. The Royal Marines were roaring around in little rubber boats underneath and I was out of the water in ten seconds.'

The Cranwell report on the graduate was couched in mellow phrases. The Prince of Wales 'will make an excellent fighter pilot at supersonic speeds ... a natural aptitude for flying ... excelled at aerobatics in jets ... all-round ability'. At the passing-out parade on August 20th, the Prince looked nervous on receiving his pilot's wings from the Air Chief Marshal, as if conscious that his father, in the uniform of Marshal of the R.A.F., was among the onlookers. The band played melodies from *Oklahoma*, with *God Save the Prince of Wales* and then a medley of Scottish airs in compliment to Charles' flat-mate, Flying Officer Gavin Mackay, who – as I have been recommended to advise you – all but swept the board of flying prizes and took much of the attention that day as the outstanding cadet of the year.

III

In signing his R.A.F. papers, the Prince of Wales had requested that he should receive no pay, a suggestion that, as an ever-watchful Palace accountant soon reminded him, had the real and actual effect of diverting a useful sum from charity. When signing on for three to five years in the Royal Navy, the Prince's solicitors amended this by drawing up a deed of gift to switch his pay and allowances to the King George's Fund for Sailors, which would produce the useful effect of passing about £11,000 to the central fund of all naval charities within five years.

'I hope I won't be too seasick. I'll stock up on seasickness pills,' Charles had clowned, on the announcement eighteen months earlier that he would follow his father, his grandfather, his great-grandfather and his great-uncle 'Dickie' into the Navy. 'Going to sea is not purely a military operation, it is a professional one,' Prince Philip had explained the preference. 'Altogether you live in a highly technological atmosphere, probably a good introduction to the kind of thing which controls our whole existence. And aboard ship you learn to live with people, that is the important thing.'

Charles was obviously well genned-up on that. He left Balmoral in mid-September, eager to put his Aston Martin through her paces on the 500-mile drive south to Dartmouth. A top greeting party, consisting of the Commander-in-Chief of Naval Home Command, the Deputy Lieutenant of Devon, the Mayor of Dartmouth and Captain Allan Tait, captain of the Royal Naval College, would be waiting to welcome him at ten a.m. on September 15th. But in reality Prince Charles arrived without fuss the previous evening to move into his 'cabin' and dine privately with Captain Tait, whom he already knew slightly.

Once again the Prince enrolled under a Graduate Entry scheme with the rank of Sub-Lieutenant but, remembering the naval dormitory tried out in Gordonstoun days, he appears to have been pleasantly surprised by Cabin A30, one of the better rooms on the first floor of the College buildings, with wide windows overlooking the vista of the river Dart. A broad, flat-topped desk stood beneath the window, with small armchairs and a standard-issue coffee table 'for reading with your feet up'. Yet the initial course was to last only six weeks and, as a navigation instructor summed up, this implied 'a heck of a lot to learn in a very short time' before Prince Charles joined the guided missile destroyer *Norfolk* for nine months at sea.

Meanwhile, the quiet dinner with Captain Tait had a setting

of personal interest, for the Captain's house was the proverbial scene of Prince Philip's first meeting with the then Princess Elizabeth during a visit with her parents. 'Nineteen years before my time,' Charles had quipped. Now it saw a turning point in his own life and the prelude to the most demanding and intensive period of study he had ever known. As the welcoming dignitaries gathered next morning on the steps of the College, the Prince left C block by a back way and, wearing naval uniform for the first time, he was driven round to the front where, dead pan, he shook Captain Tait's hand and announced, 'I've had a long drive, sir.'

The introductions included his tutor, Mr M. K. Armistead, and three graduates of his own age, respectively from Buxton, Glasgow and Gibraltar, who would be sharing the same course. The basic professional training of the next six weeks included seamanship, navigation, marine and electrical engineering and the 'man management' duties of a divisional officer, together with practical work on the college minesweeper *Walkerton*. Also, for the first time, the Prince experienced an evident personal anxiety in the outcome, in having much to live up to. In 1939 his father had won the King's Dirk as the best special entry cadet of the year. His 'Uncle Dickie' Mountbatten, in another generation, had come top out of eighty in the final exams.

For his six-week stint Prince Charles worked with the same family intensity of application. His day began at six a.m. with studies until 'pipe down' at ten thirty p.m., and time off was limited to crewing once or twice in a Flying Dutchman, sessions on the squash court – where he was eager to be coached – and some weekend swimming with friends in Cornwall, who remember him 'swotting at naval manuals, lying on the beach'. Persistence brought its due reward for, as Lord Mountbatten said, 'My great-nephew was top in navigation and top in seamanship, and that is all we seamen care about.'

On the day of the passing-out parade Prince Philip was in Berlin and Princess Anne even more distantly occupied, blowing up an ancient bus on a firing-range north of Hong Kong with the regiment of which she is Colonel-in-Chief. Charles was pointedly on his own until the last moment when, as Admiral of the Fleet, Earl Mountbatten telephoned Captain Tait to say, 'I think the family should be represented, so I'm flying down.' After the march-past, it added zest for Charles to take off in the 'chopper' with his Uncle Dickie, flying home in time to lunch with the Queen at the Palace. Only a day or two later, the Prince was in Wales to attend a conservation conference at Merthyr Tydfil and see for himself some of the tidying-up projects in the neighbourhood. The following week, he again took part in the State Opening of Parliament. Not a dull moment.

IV

In 1971–72 H.M.S. *Norfolk* was the latest of five guided missile destroyers belonging to the Royal Navy, a grey 5,600-tonner destined to contribute to the NATO standing naval force in the North Atlantic. In the late autumn of 1971, however, her immediate mission concerned exercises in the Mediterranean to which Sub-Lieutenant Prince Charles was assigned while working for his naval certificate of competence and his watch-keeping certificate. While awaiting his posting the Prince noted, with an inherited touch of King George VI's interest in heraldry, that the ship's crest was 'a silver ostrich feather with a gold quill ensigned by a gold prince's coronet, the pen piercing a scroll bearing the motto *Ich Dien*'. The crest derived from the insignia of a previous battleship *Norfolk*, and was based in turn on the county badge, but the improbable coincidence remained. A coincidence, too, that the Prince flew out to Gibraltar to join the ship on November 5th, the commemoration day of Guy Fawkes, 'a fiendishly chosen date', as Charles asserted with a grin.

Thus, in taking up his active life in the Senior Service, he again stepped into a new world, a world of layered dimensions like the painted glass slides in a Japanese peepshow. In the foreground was the wide field of diplomatic and political history of which the heir to the throne formed a part, a role so paramount in many eyes that the good people of Gibraltar had hoped he would undertake a ceremonial drive through the streets and the Foreign Ministry in Madrid officially lodged a note of protest that the Prince's visit to the Rock 'unnecessarily hurt national feeling and stirred up Spanish public opinion'. Simultaneously, in Whitehall, there were Ministry of Defence advisers who considered it undesirable that H.M.S. *Norfolk*, and Prince Charles, should put into Malta at a time of politically sensitive negotiations with the island's government. If the Prince felt irritation, it was justified on the ground that Malta's premier, Mr Dom Mintoff, was already a friend with whom he enjoyed most cordial relations. Among such curiosities of protocol even H.M.S. *Norfolk's* future commitments to NATO posed difficulties lest, if Prince Charles were aboard, the numerous visits to NATO ports might appear to foreign dignitaries as tantamount to a royal tour.

At this regal level Charles found a crowd waiting to give him a cheer at Gibraltar airport and he was piped aboard H.M.S. *Norfolk* and greeted by its commanding officer. But as a green Sub-Lieutenant he had flown out on a trooper and a naval Land-Rover drove him to the dock. Introductions, drinks in the wardroom, tinkling ice breaking the ice, and meanwhile the British Embassy in Madrid was making it clear that 'His Royal Highness' movements as a serving officer are subject to normal operational requirements and are purely a matter for Her Majesty's Government.'

And so the Prince's personal world shrank into Cabin 36 starboard on 01 deck, a space seven feet by seven feet from porthole to the back of the steel washbasin, from bunkhead to sliding door wardrobe, the bunk a cat-leap above the drawers and the desk, and the porthole ledge serving as a shelf for family photographs, the more non-committal the better. Headphones on a hook from the record-player, and cramped remaining space to study the Midshipman's Task Book or compile the Junior Officer's Journal. A pleasant change, nevertheless, that no police detective dogged his heels, for at sea the Royal Navy accepted responsibility for security, and detectives would be flown out for shore duties only as necessary. The food, too, was unexpectedly good, for the ship had just won the Navy's annual cookery contest, first out of two hundred entries. Taken on a midshipman's first inspection tour below decks, the Prince asked a chef where he had learned to cook and received the unexpected response, 'In part, at Buckingham Palace, sir.' Naval chefs needing experience of larger galleys had been taking a two-month course in the Palace kitchens.

H.M.S. *Norfolk* sailed on November 6th, the ceaseless vibration of the engines heralding the bustle of the self-contained community so familiar to Prince Philip, so comparatively unfamiliar to his eldest son. Prince Charles found himself in effect an apprentice in the machinery control room, a junior assistant at the steering wheel on 2 deck and presently as second officer sharing the watch on the bridge. Nine days out, somewhere in the Mediterranean, he noted his twenty-third birthday, a day with no more than two mystery packages to unwrap from his baggage and no birthday cards, the wardroom being as yet uncertain of protocol. An uneventful voyage, it may have seemed, to the more experienced. For Sub-Lieutenant Prince Charles the main adventure was being on watch during a force ten gale off Sardinia, the incessant ping of the sonar assuming an unexpected quality of drama amid the uproar of the storm.

Home in time for Christmas at Windsor and, early in the New Year of 1972, back in Portsmouth for the ship's dance at the Locarno ballroom, an epic scene for the bandsmen who watched Charles gaily swinging it with officers' wives and girl friends.

Another highlight that January was the familiarisation course in submarines, normal in all Sub-Lieutenants' training, which involved a practice emergency escape from the bottom of the hundred-foot training tank at Gosport. At prior hints that this might be foregone the Prince had expressed himself tersely, something like 'Not on your Nellie'. Five thousand officers and men passed through the escape tank every year. Princes are less frequent and the event became an elaborate exercise in recruitment and public relations, involving naval and civil press photographers, arc-lamps, the full treatment.

Earl Mountbatten recalled a precedent of sixty years ago when King George V and his second son (King George VI) had dived and covered three nautical miles in the submarine D.4. It was no less personally exciting for the Prince of Wales to make his three escapes, from thirty feet, sixty feet and a hundred feet, no breathing apparatus involved. Leaving the airlock, the essential drill is to breathe out, 'whistle on the way up', fifteen seconds to bounce to the surface. 'Incredible!' gasped Charles, emerging goggled and nose-clipped. The following month the Prince undertook a twenty-four-hour patrol in the nuclear submarine *Churchill*, beneath the sea off the Scottish coast, again with benefit for the recruitment cameras ... 'Prince Charles operates the sub's diving controls .. The Prince at the periscope.' But for everyone concerned it would have seemed less simple if one could have known that within two years two trainees would lose their lives in escape tank accidents.

Though realising that he was being pushed through 'a shortened course of introduction to the Navy', the Prince also recognised the heightened responsibility. 'I have to try that little bit harder to be as professional as possible ... to assimilate all the vast problems rather more quickly.' He was keenly aware of the *pace*, and the substantial programmes that other people had mapped out, with the solid difficulty that he was sometimes expected to achieve the impossible. Feeling that he would benefit from immediate experience of a smaller ship, his mentors switched him for three weeks to the Fleet Air Arm frigate

Hermione while H.M.S. *Norfolk* was under 'self-maintenance' at Portsmouth. In March, he was put through as much action as possible, both against a pretended enemy and during an earth-quake relief landing in the republic of Portlandia.

In realistic terms, the naval base at Portland was staging a working-up exercise in conjunction with NATO in which H.M.S. *Norfolk* and other ships put to sea to run the gauntlet of submarine and torpedo-boat attacks. On the morning of March 8th Prince Charles was transferred to one of the smallest and fastest of the attackers, the gas-turbine craft *Scimitar*, then under the command of the youngest skipper in the Navy, twenty-five-year-old Lieutenant Paul Haddacks. After a day of getting to know the vessel, the Prince slept in the cramped wardroom top bunk, a fact still proudly commemorated by a small typed card on the bulkhead, and next day he took the wheel in earnest against the defending warships, skimming the craft across the waves with all the thrust of her 7,000 horsepower engines, and swerving sharply away after the mock torpedo attack behind a dense smoke-screen. The following week, the Prince was with an earthquake relief party making its way to a derelict wartime army camp not many miles from Portland, where there were 'dead' lying in the streets and the situation was aggravated by 'looters'.

But his 'very glamorous romantic idea about the Navy wasn't always borne out', as he once reported. There were also 'an awful lot of mundane tasks', and when H.M.S. *Norfolk* next sailed for NATO exercises in the Mediterranean, it came as a relief that fewer fine points of diplomatic sensitivity arose to cramp his style. The Queen and Prince Philip were just then paying a state visit to France, Charles had long urged his mother to try to include Provence in her itinerary and, thanks to a strategic leave pass, mother and son were able to see Avignon together and the royal party spent the night at the famed Baumanière Hotel near the steep and strange hill-town of Les Baux. By the afternoon President Pompidou's official plane had whisked them to Paris for the Longchamp races, and that evening Charles was dancing energetically at the British Embassy, which can really do these things in style.

It had been Emma Soames' idea that there should be a 'young people's dance' of at least a hundred couples in the garden pavilion, and her parents, Sir Christopher and Lady Soames, carried out the scheme admirably.

Then, as sailors must, Charles had to return to his ship. From Toulon, H.M.S. *Norfolk* cruised uneventfully to Ajaccio, where the Prince and a dozen shipmates piled into a mini-bus to explore the blue granite regions inland. Next evening, when the destroyer invited local notabilities for cocktails, the mayor did a nice doubletake on discovering that one of the two welcoming officers at the gangplank was Prince Charles. During the weekend in Malta, the Prince contacted Dom Mintoff and the two got on famously, spending a morning water-skiing together and lunching at the Premier's country home.

Sadly, the Malta visit was curtailed by the death of the Duke of Windsor, and the recall of Prince Charles home to Windsor for the funeral. A year or two earlier, when spending a weekend in Paris with Nicholas Soames, Charles had characteristically foregone other diversions to pay a surprise call on his great-uncle, a kindly act that had given the ailing old man and his Duchess great pleasure. Not ten days ago, Prince Charles had visited him again in Paris with the Queen; the Duke had been too ill to come downstairs and they had talked of Provence for a little in his upstairs sitting-room. Now the former Prince of Wales was dead, and there was only the sorrow and the significance of the tragedy of a Prince who had perhaps not married in time and of a King who had loved the wrong woman.

On Saturday June 3rd the Duchess drove to Windsor to see her husband lying in state, and it was Prince Charles who gently led her into St George's Chapel and supported her as she gazed at the catafalque. 'Thirty-five years,' she said, again and again, and it was indeed thirty-five years since her wedding day.

10   Prince of All Trades

I

On a sunny day at the end of June, 1972, the Queen visited the destroyer *Norfolk* at Portsmouth 'while I still have the chance', as she said. 'Will it be convenient?' the Prince of Wales had asked Captain J. W. D. Cook. The visit signalled the close of the Prince's training with H.M.S. *Norfolk*, where he had latterly become assistant to the guided missiles officer. On leaving the ship in July, there followed a brief communications course in the naval signals school, *Mercury*, in the hills above Petersfield, as well as other qualifying courses, from bridge-keeping to nuclear defence, at her neighbouring establishment *Dryad*. The Prince talked naval fashion of Pompey, the fond local term for Portsmouth, and found time for polo at Midhurst and Windsor, haring back and forth in his nippy Aston Martin.

This was the year when Princess Anne was disappointed – by the withdrawal of her horse Doublet – in her hopes of riding in the British Olympics team at Munich. To help brighten her spirits, Charles teased her by claiming that he hoped to play for Britain and, sure enough, with mock fanfares by State trumpeters of the Household Cavalry, he led a Young British polo team onto Smith's Lawn at Windsor to try their strength against the Young Americans, only to face disastrous defeat. But there's always a next time, he reminded the victors. It was the summer also when he attended the country wedding of his twenty-seven-year-old cousin, Prince Richard of Gloucester, arriving by 'chopper' with his grandmother, and Charles blithely responded to jests on his own romantic chances by saying that there were three years to go before being Richard's age.

Then, only a month after the wedding, Richard's elder bachelor brother, Prince William, was tragically killed when his light plane crashed during an air race. Before the family could recover from the first dreadful shock, it happened that Prince Charles was due to take a Cranwell refresher course under arrangements made months beforehand, and that a Jet Provost Mark 7, the type of aircraft he would be flying, had crashed only the previous week. Life had to go on, but the Queen was understandably as tense as in the days when Prince Philip had first started flying helicopters and she had made sure that the Household doctor had a key to the locked gate between his surgery and the landing site in the Palace gardens.

The records show that Prince Charles satisfactorily flew the Mark 7 aeroplane, as well as the new Hunter high-speed jet fighter. Next, he returned to Portland for a short course with the coastal mine-sweeper *Glasserton*. But of more personal importance, he took a week's course in helicopter flying at the naval air training base at Yeovilton and scarcely realised at the time that he had hit upon perhaps the most compelling interest of his naval and flying career.

The Prince once said good-humouredly that he was a Jack-of-all-trades – soldier, sailor, airman, conservationist, speaker at public dinners . . . and in October, following the state visit of President and Frau Heinemann of Federal Germany to the Queen at Windsor, he changed into military uniform and flew to Berlin to attend the training sessions of three infantry battalions of the Prince of Wales Division. Visiting Osnabruck for the St David's Day celebration of his Royal Regiment of Wales the previous year he had, as a new officer, followed Mess tradition by eating a raw leek and singing a song unaccompanied – his choice was, of course, the Goon song – and he had watched with sympathy as other new entrants suffered a leek-eating race. But now the Prince was guest of honour at a reception held by the West Berlin Senate, a symptom, he said, of his progress through the mill. From Berlin he then flew direct to Malaga for a few days' shooting on the Wellesley estate with his army friend Arthur Wellesley, the Marquess of Douro, the Duke of Wellington's son and heir, a brief holiday that proved the first zephyr in the hurricane of unwise surmise that he might marry Arthur's younger sister, Lady Jane Wellesley.

He was home in good time for his twenty-fourth birthday, when one of his friends made up a theatre party of four couples to see Noël Coward's *Cowardy Custard* at the Mermaid: there was safety in numbers. Soldier, sailor, airman, actor, clown . . . 'It's a pity I had to give up acting,' Charles sighed to Bernard Miles. But the band played Happy Birthday, the audience applauded and the Prince irresistibly stood up and took a bow.

II

'Prince Charles and Princess Anne request the pleasure of your company . . .' ran the invitation to the private supper party for the Queen and Prince Philip's silver wedding anniversary on November 20th, six days after that Mermaid ovation. Charles fretted and frowned over the guest-list, anxious that no one who had been close to his parents through twenty-five years should be omitted. He remembered to ask the new Poet Laureate, Sir John Betjeman, to write a poem to the Queen, which was delivered by hand to the Palace but which has never been published. He commissioned a piece of contemporary silver with an inscription from all four of the Queen's children, without omitting to collect a proportionate subscription from eight-year-old Prince Edward. He discreetly made sure that both his brothers would be home from Heatherdown School, in case that detail should be overlooked. And early on their silver wedding day the Queen and Prince Philip were serenaded by a barber-shop quartet giving a spirited family rendering with trumpet and drums of *Happy Anniversary*.

Princess Anne once said comically of Charles, 'We live in the same house and have rooms at opposite ends of a corridor. But we usually go out at different times. The only time I see a lot of him is during holidays – and roughly speaking that's enough.' She meant not a word of it, and all six of the family were together for the 'Anniversary of the Marriage', as the *Court Circular* put it. Prince Andrew and Prince Edward attended the Westminster Abbey service of thanksgiving and only afterwards retired for nursery lunch and television. Prince Charles successfully kidded some of the Palace staff that he was preparing a speech for the Guildhall luncheon, and no one dreamed of the pains he took over a highly amusing but apparently impromptu speech in proposing his parents' health that evening. For Charles at least the only dull moment of the day was the royal walkabout that afternoon through the Barbican, which he privately considered 'a complete concrete jungle ... rather depressing'. But he was in good form in his quips to the crowd: 'That's all I need,' pointing to a sign *Drug Store*, 'someone to photograph me under it' and, to a group of City typists, 'Are you the girls who sit on the boss's knee?'

There had rarely been a happier, more congenial assembly of royalty and friends than the party that evening; Buckingham Palace was floodlit and looking quite magical. The Queen and Prince Philip had originally thought of a small dinner party. Instead, Charles and Anne had succeeded in keeping much of the preparation secret beforehand, and the State dining-room and supper room had never glowed with truer richness and gaiety. Not least, the 'entertainment' in the ballroom showed the Prince's own unmistakable touch, with the English Chamber Orchestra to open the concert with the Wedding March and part of the Bach Choir to recall the anthems of the wedding service.

Some claim with good reason that the romance between Princess Anne and Lieutenant Mark Phillips began that evening. Lady Abergavenny had also been with the Queen 'in waiting' throughout the day, and among some two hundred guests the

Nevills, Hesse-Hanovers and Wernhers formed three of the larger family groups.

That same week, the Prince of Wales joined his new ship, the frigate *Minerva*, at Portsmouth. The intention was that he should now gain experience in a small general-purpose ship where he would shoulder more responsibility, and the frigate's seventeen officers were a close-knit and congenial company. After a mission to Antwerp with the Prince as a newcomer, the ship was fogbound for two days in the busy Thames estuary waiting to dock at Chatham, and the wardroom kidded him that it was all his fault. 'I get a good deal of ribbing,' he once acknowledged. 'Half the battle is to give as good as you get.' Three Aussie sub-lieutenants who once shared an instruction course had shown him little mercy. 'Little did they know I had only to blow my whistle to have them thrown into the Tower!' said Charles at the farewell dinner. At which he blew a whistle, and by prior arrangement in marched three Yeomen of the Guard . . .

In the New Year of 1973 H.M.S. *Minerva* was placed on a six-month commission in the West Indies, and Prince Charles sailed with her in mid-February, with new cause for exhilaration, for his private brief on the voyage had been widened to comprise new tasks of diplomacy with his naval duties. Unlike the Prince of Wales of a century ago, this Prince had no grounds for complaint that he was given nothing to do, though his personal security so far from home soon aroused acute Cabinet concern in London. The first stop was Bermuda, where it seemed sensible that the Prince should spend his shore-leave at Government House to have time to discuss with the Governor, Sir Richard Sharples, many of the interlocking problems arising from the forthcoming independence of the neighbouring Bahamas. The two men conferred until a late hour and then went for a late-night stroll in the gardens where, on just such a stroll barely a week later, Sir Richard and a young aide were shot dead by an unknown assassin.

H.M.S. *Minerva*, with Prince Charles, had set sail by then
for Puerto Rico, but there remained the disquieting thought that
in planning his evil purpose the killer may well have lurked in
the shadows close to the Prince. The frigate was due to return
to Bermuda for essential maintenance and, partly to avoid the
extra burden on the widowed Lady Sharples, Prince Charles
was temporarily transferred to the survey ship *Fox*, based on
Antigua. As an assistant navigating officer on this small (800-
ton) hydrographic vessel, he thus found himself satisfyingly
involved in the attempts to refloat the huge Swedish bulk
carrier *Ariadne* which, nearly as large as the liner *Queen Elizabeth 2*, had grounded on a reef in the coral-strewn waters.

At Easter, the Brabournes had invited him to feel at home to
use their beach house on Windermere Island in the Bahamas,
and he revelled in a brief holiday of scuba-diving and sunning.
Making the most of time as well as place is an ingrained royal
talent. At the end of May, he flew home to join the family
at Balmoral for Princess Anne's engagement to Lieutenant Mark
Phillips; it was equally an occasion to consult the Queen, whom
he was to represent at the Bahamas independence celebrations
in July. In the following week he was due to open the restored
fortifications of the Prince of Wales Bastion at St Kitts, but
he nevertheless utilised a Jamaica stopover on the return flight
for a match with the Kingston Polo Club.

And so back to H.M.S. *Minerva* where, promoted Lieutenant,
he was presently second gunnery officer. During manoeuvres,
the 4.5-inch guns and Seacat missiles of the frigate were now
more than familiar armament, and their care and maintenance
became his personal responsibility, as naval duties and discipline
alternated with the Caribbean pleasures of shore-leave. Prince
Charles' ship was inevitably the most popular vessel afloat.
Invitations were never lacking: at Montserrat the bubbling hot
springs could scarcely be seen for sailors and, during the week
of independence celebrations in the Bahamas, every man aboard
seemed to be adopted by a Nassau family. During the course

of the ceremonies one of Charles' goonish comic visions came true, luckily without harm, when an awning collapsed over the tiers of official guests – picture-hats were rammed over ladies' ears by tumbling microphones, and morning-coated dignitaries and the judiciary in wigs and gowns disappeared from view beneath the canvas. At a State ball given by the new self-governing regime, the guests backed away to watch the Prince performing a pulsating local dance known as the merengue. 'If I hear rhythmic music I just want to get up and dance,' Charles told Kenneth Harris of *The Observer*. 'That's one of the reasons why I had such a marvellous time in the West Indies.'

No shortage of description, then, in his long letters home, and naturally it was more the diversions than the duties that sped his pen. There had been fascinating diving in the Virgin Islands, 'diving on a wreck of 1867,' as the Prince wrote, 'and experiencing the extraordinary sensation of some vast green cathedral filled with shoals of silver fish.' In Portsmouth, New Hampshire, the ship's company attended 'a whale of a reception' for the 350th anniversary of the town. The farthest south they ventured was a port in the Gulf of Venezuela, visited on the joyous excuse that the Prince should take part in the re-enactment of a civil war naval battle of a hundred and fifty years ago, and in the same latitudes this adventure was satisfyingly capped by the aqualung diving off Cartagena, where the Prince explored the underwater hulk of a seventeenth-century Spanish wreck and emerged triumphantly grasping two silver pieces of eight.

III

Prince Charles will probably never get to know his fellow men better than aboard H.M.S. *Minerva*, and his fellows will never know the man behind the Prince better than during the unguarded intimacy of the long days at sea. The officers came from every part of the British Isles and two from the Antipodes, from every level of society from grammar school up. One by one Prince Charles learned their personal life stories, and heard tales of wives, girl friends and parents. Confidences were shared, snapshots produced, letters sometimes read out ... every man is a fortress but drawbridges were lowered under the euphoria of the boundless ocean. In Halifax, Nova Scotia, Charles was taken to see someone's aunt, sitting down to supper Canadian style in the kitchen. Questions were asked at deeper levels of candour. Wouldn't he like a life of his own? 'But I do have a life of my own,' the Prince protested. Wouldn't he like to be free? 'Free from what?' Charles would counter.

In these conversational treasure-hunts he felt it important to be as honest and genuine as possible. Some men could always see through you if you were faking, sailors especially. Didn't he want to be free to mix with other people? 'A fallacy that I don't mix,' Charles protested. 'We're mixing now. But none of us can mix with, say, people in different jobs all the time.' An incisive question might be parried: at the very core of a heart-to-heart conversation the other chap would meet an iron wall of absolute discretion. 'We learned a lot about Prince Charles – nothing whatever about the Queen or even his sister!' one officer summed up. Glancing over the royal photographs in his cabin, another shipmate ventured, 'What, no girls?' Charles simply said, 'Climb up on my bunk. They're behind the bulkhead shaft.' And there they were, five or six lovelies, but the Prince made no comment on their identities, giving nothing away, 'and something in his eye, you know, forbade one to ask.' And there was the moment of truth, the end of a very happy chapter, as everyone realised, when H.M.S. *Minerva* docked at Chatham in September at the end of a seven-month tour.

The Prince was due to be posted to the frigate *Jupiter* in January, and no one thought it odd that one of his first home duties ashore was a regimental inspection. He had, in fact, included a personal report to the Royal Regiment of Wales among his letters home from the Caribbean, 'I thought if it interests me to read about what's going on with them, it might interest them to read about what's going on with me.' More than this, he had discovered on visiting the regiment in Germany that the soldiers couldn't always make themselves understood by the German girls. So he had suggested supplying them with a special phrase book of 'getting togetherness' and had begun jotting down useful phrases as soon as he returned to his aircraft. 'Not that they really needed my German,' he said. 'But I had promised it and they could see that I kept my word.'

For those four months at home that autumn, Prince Charles seemed to me to be doing everything at the double. One knows that he had firmly asked his secretary, Squadron-Leader David Checketts, to book him up to the limit, making up for lost time after the months at sea, and his engagement books bristled with interpolations and insertions. During the Queen's journey to Australia to open the Sydney Opera House, the Prince acted as a Counsellor of State and, among other tasks undertaken at the Palace for the first time, he welcomed and accepted letters of credence from the new ambassadors, a time-saving and useful function on his mother's behalf. Among his foremost private pre-occupations was Princess Anne's impending wedding. The romance, as we have seen, had burgeoned during his absence overseas, and Charles felt that he needed time to get to know Mark Phillips better. The evenings afforded occasion for two or three pleasant little dinner parties given at the Palace by brother and sister. Mark was less than two months older than Charles; they had often met at Badminton and Eridge and now the two found they shared a mutual interest in shooting, among other country pastimes they had in common. Skilfully taking up this topic, Charles soon decided to give his future brother-in-law two leather gun cases as a wedding present.

Charles' wedding gift to Anne needed deeper consideration. Diamonds are forever, and ultimately he chose a diamond brooch of great beauty, blending five ribbon loops terminating in diamond set tassels, the centre a cluster of diamonds, all set in silver and gold. At the State Opening of Parliament, Charles and Anne rode alone with the Queen in the Irish State Coach, probably the last time they would be together in this way in ceremonial. The Prince wore naval uniform for the first time at a State Opening and it was typical of his energetic programme that, having changed into mufti, he took off from the Palace by helicopter immediately after lunch to open a new police head-quarters in Huntingdon.

Again, there were journeys to Wales to deliver the conservation speeches he had written at sea, to Bristol to inaugurate a new water scheme, to the Scilly Isles and then to Somerset to attend a harvest thanksgiving in his role as Duke of Cornwall. One busy day, he followed engagements in Luxemburg with an evening charity function for the Lord's Taverners in London. 'I've always wondered how it feels to do two shows a night,' he told Jimmy Edwards. Meanwhile, in the romantic atmosphere of Mark and Anne, one noticed that newspaper editors were longing for a matching love-story around the Prince. They snatched at incidents like greedy children, as when Charles flew off for four days shooting on the Duke of Wellington's estate in Spain, and conjectures gathered afresh around the Duke's daughter, Lady Jane Wellesley. The cameramen jostled when Charles visited the Alhambra by moonlight (or flash-bulb) with a dozen of the Dukes' guests and the amiable Jane. 'Bronzed and happy they flew home together,' one newspaper announced, although it might have been added that ten other members of the house-party were in the same plane.

Upset on seeing the glowing headlines, Charles lost no time in attempting to telephone Jane to express his sympathy and apologies . . . yet their friendship was in fact still at such a mild stage that he had to ring her brother for her Fulham telephone number. The Wellesleys were New Year guests at Sandringham by way of return hospitality, but at the gates of the estate a crowd estimated at ten thousand waited to catch a glimpse of the royal family and of Jane in particular, an unwelcome and over-vivid instance all round of the difficulties of the flowery path.

Mercifully for all concerned the sensation was short-lived. In the dawn of January 2nd – 'a fiendish time of day', as he said – Prince Charles flew off on a trooping plane from Brize Norton to join his new ship, H.M.S. *Jupiter*, in Singapore.

IV

The frigate *Jupiter* was of the same Leander class as *Minerva*, and the fact that Prince Charles was soon lost to sight in the Java Sea was relative. As with their sister ship, the crew found themselves gifted with regal status at every anchorage, the most sought after, most questioned and necessarily the most discreet sailors afloat. It was for a navy promotional department in Whitehall to publicise any adventure of attractive general interest. The Prince was communications officer of the watch south-west of Macassar on a night of driving rain when distress signals were received from the tug *Mediator* which had gone aground with two barges in tow. The warship's Wasp helicopter took off to locate the stranded vessels and, after a boarding party was landed on one of the barges in the torrential and blinding downpour, all three were pulled clear and towed to safety, an epic for all concerned.

An uneventful voyage in calm seas followed to Brisbane, where Charles dashed the seventy miles to Mooloolaba Beach while on shore-leave to go surfing on 'the best boomers around'. 'One was never far from home,' he told guests at the cocktail party given by *Jupiter*, and it indeed seemed so when, with a glance at his watch, he raced into a suburban police station next evening to 'phone his father at the Williamstown R.A.A.F. base north of Sydney where Prince Philip was stopping over on his way to open the Commonwealth Games in New Zealand.

This was at the height of a rush period of more than usually congested royal schedules and itineraries. Prince Philip in-augurated the Games on January 24th. The Queen and the young wedded pair, Princess Anne and Mark Phillips, flew out from London on January 27th to pay a twenty-eight-hour visit to Rarotonga, in the Cook Islands, and were on time for their engagements in Christchurch on January 30th. When H.M.S. *Jupiter* docked at Christchurch at dawn on the 29th, Philip was aboard the *Britannia* moored six berths away, and Charles sprinted the dockside railway lines towards the royal yacht at such speed that some said he had set his heart on the jape of carrying in his father's early morning tea.

Before the Queen and Prince Philip left Auckland in the royal yacht with Anne and Mark, Charles, aboard *Jupiter*, had already left for Suva, Samoa, Hawaii, and the Fijian isle of Bega where he took part with the islanders in the swimming technique of driving the fish forward into nets – 'like a submerged pheasant drive.' When the royal family were in the New Hebrides, he requested permission as communications officer to radio greetings from the same latitude. One next heard of him in San Diego where no Prince of Wales had been seen for fifty-four years and where, had he wished to cash in on popularity, he could have accepted a kiss from Shami the whale, enjoyed the free use of a $500-a-night hotel penthouse and could have been kitted out with a home-knitted set of stars-and-stripes underwear. In pre-ference, however, the British Consul-General thought it best to announce that the Prince was undergoing serious naval training and would accept no social engagements.

If this were not quite true, the diplomatic excuse served to ensure a rapid all-round glimpse of California. Seven British naval officers went to eat in an English-style restaurant, and then became aware that everyone at every table was standing up to look at the seventh man, Prince Charles. Walter Annenberg, who was then U.S. ambassador in London, entertained him at the family Palm Springs estate – one of the rare occasions when the Prince played golf – and shore leave also included sightseeing in the Hollywood studios, sipping tea with Barbra Streisand at Columbia and driving through the trick parting of the Red Sea at Universal, 'great for a car wash', as the Prince said.

Then there was a real American blonde in the person of an Admiral's daughter, Laura Jo Watkins, tanned and twenty and glossy-lipped, who monopolised Charles for fifteen minutes at a yacht club party and so found herself in the local news. 'Why, Laura Jo is a lovely young woman,' announced a family friend to the converging reporters. 'Any relationship with a gentleman would certainly end in marriage.' Whereupon three months later Laura Jo actually flew to London to attend a party given by the Annenbergs, at which Charles was not present, and to see him give his maiden speech in the House of Lords. For the next three days she faced a furore of headlines and speculation and then she flew home, somewhat embarrassed, back to the American dream. A curious episode.

Despite palpitating hearts and bulkhead photographs, it was the way of the world to note that nothing marred the celibate escutcheon. There were other pastimes. Four months in the Pacific meant reading Solzhenitsyn's *The Gulag Archipelago* and Woodham-Smith's *Queen Victoria*, besides drafting future speeches, writing one or two book prefaces and 'doing a not very spectacular job surrounded by miles and miles of sea'. One week, the Prince directed a flight deck entertainment and was a distinct hit of the show himself as a slapstick drinks dispenser. At times, finding a quiet corner on a torpid afternoon, he took up his absorbing old hobby of water-colour painting, 'difficult but most rewarding' as he found it, though unconvinced of his personal skill.

Edward Seago, the Norfolk artist, had once given him a lesson, dashing off from memory a 'marvellous little picture of two Thames barges'. Charles asked if he might keep this and he still regards it as a cherished personal possession. His own pictures he lightly dismisses as 'jolly useful for Christmas presents', impressionistic studies of the Panama Canal locks or perhaps a market

group on the docks, but sketches of the *Jupiter*'s Wasp helicopter
appear like a recurrent hieroglyph, a symbol of escape and longing
that might interest the psychologist.

From Panama on, it fell to Prince Charles, as a flight deck
officer, to signal the helicopter for launching or touch-down, and
the prospect of a helicopter course with the Fleet Air Arm
opened as the next desirable objective. When his ship returned
home to Devonport, there was not only a minibus bearing a
placard 'H.M. Tower of London for officers of H.M.S. Jupiter'
but also an expected posse of press cameramen. The Prince suggested that it would be a good idea if he could be seen doing one
of his everyday jobs, such as waving his bats to guide the helicopter for launching, and his captain agreed. 'It made a change
for the photographers,' said Charles. 'It was more typical and it
was the truth.'

V

Enter a dragon, a dragon in a red coat. Throughout the summer
of 1974, Prince Charles told anyone who would listen how much
he was looking forward to flying helicopters. After batting the
chopper, the next step was flying one solo, and after becoming
operationally qualified, to use the jargon, one had the useful
freedom of the air, unless the Cabinet should spoil everything
by over-caution. Hence the dragon, the call-sign from Cranwell
dredged up in new guise as the Red Dragon of Wales. The
Prince approved the scarlet and gold dragon arm-flashes of his
training unit with much pleasure. His three and a half month
instruction would be at the Royal Naval Air Station at Yeovilton,
Somerset, scene of his first dual-control chopper flights, and he
bubbled with elation. 'I can't think of a better combination, being
at sea and being able to fly,' he remarked, putting his finger on
the pulse of the daydream.

His father had become a qualified helicopter pilot at the ripe
age of thirty-five. Charles at twenty-five could teasingly promise

to beat him by nearly ten years. During his first month at Yeovilton he had occasion to change out of denims into full uniform to tap a mallet on a block of stone, laying the foundation stone of the new Fleet Air Arm Museum, and he asked, 'Will you have anything of my father's?' But they couldn't yet be sure on that. Prince Philip had pioneered royal choppers and taken off from the lawns of Buckingham Palace in a naval helicopter, as a passenger, in Coronation Year. As a student flyer, Charles now faced ground instruction of fifty-three hours, dual instruction of thirty-eight hours and fifteen hours of solo flight as minimum requirements, not in precisely that progression. The Prince said afterwards that he had found the course easier and gained the knack more quickly than he had thought.

There were more things to do than in fixed-wing aircraft, one had to keep an inherently unstable machine under control in every aspect of vertical flight, hovering, executing manoeuvres under all weather conditions. 'You've got to expect something to go wrong any minute and be ready to do something about it pretty quickly,' Prince Charles put the gist of it. He first flew solo in a Wessex 5 Commando ten days after first handling the controls, about average for a jet pilot. But comfortably before Christmas he achieved a hundred and four flying hours, twenty-six of them solo, in forty-five days, quite a hard flying rate in the opinion of the station commander, Lieutenant Commander P. A. Voute.

About halfway through the tuition there was inserted 'with fiendish cunning' a Royal Marines assault and survival course, on the basis that since chopper pilots have to ferry Marines it's as well to understand what they have to put up with. 'You have to swing over chasms on ropes, slide down ropes at death-defying speed and then walk across wires strung between a pole and a tree,' the Prince recorded in vivid description. It reminded him of the junior perils of swinging hand over hand along the rope over the lake at Gordonstoun, except that one did not then have to crawl through tunnels half-filled with water and then run across the moor and back. Feeling almost too tired to stand at the end of the day, one nevertheless emerged triumphant.

He deservedly observed his twenty-sixth birthday with a day off at Buckingham Palace, and in the evening took the Queen and Princess Alexandra, and one or two others, to the theatre to see the Alan Ayckbourn comedy *Absurd Person Singular*. As he said, he liked going out to enjoy a good laugh. Back in camp, a tang of satisfaction clung to his final day of helicopter training when, among exercises in lifting and flying with an underslung load, he had the pleasure of sharing in the rescue of a cannon from the days of Nelson. Found embedded in the sands of Llanddwyn Island, and estimated to weigh a ton and a half, the gun was successfully lifted and flown to the R.A.F. field at Valley Anglesey to be cleaned and restored by the pupils of a Welsh technical school, and eventually stand on exhibition.

'What a great relief it is,' said Prince Philip, 'when you find you've actually brought up a reasonable and civilised human being,' and both men derived immense satisfaction from the continuity of their family careers. Prince Charles just then was also preparing a foreword for a new history of the Fleet Air Arm, from which the part played by hereditary strains grew ever plainer. 'Pride swells in the heart,' he wrote, 'when I recall the part played by my great-grandfather, Prince Louis of Battenberg, in the formation of the Royal Naval Air Service in 1914. Without his interest and enthusiasm and his determined support of the aeroplane versus the airship the Naval Air Service might quite literally have had great difficulty in getting off the ground.'

It was appropriate that the family successor to this tradition should be given a passing out to remember, and the Red Dragons devised much of their own ceremonial, assisted by the fact that the helicopters of 707 Squadron were also due to celebrate their tenth anniversary. With his brother officers, Charles privately celebrated the evening beforehand by visiting a pub or two in Okehampton. 'My favourite occupation is not going to pubs,' the Prince insists, but this occasion was different. 'Marvellous old boys in caps came up and said, "Like ter shake yer 'and." One old chap produced his Home Guard certificate signed by my grandfather. He'd carried it about all these years.' Yet most of the newspaper reports next day concentrated on a light-hearted search for local cider. 'Anyone would think I was an alcoholic,' the Prince regretfully told one news editor.

By way of surprise, the Yeovilton personnel presented him with a plaque bearing the air station emblem of a heron, and next day he received not only the trophy for the student making the best progress of the year but, perhaps more valued, a pen-stand made from part of a helicopter rotor blade which today has a place of honour on his Palace desk. Blending drama and pageantry, his personal standard streaming from the winch wire below his machine, the Prince then led a formation fly past of sixteen choppers, leaving trails of coloured smoke to create a rainbow across the sky.

Yet the last handshakes that signalled the end of a chapter were almost unendurable. He realised that, against all his inclinations, he had been protected against foreseeable hazard beyond the routine safety regulations. 'One does all sorts of things,' he summed up. 'Carrying commando troops, rocket firing, taking off and landing on carriers or the back end of a ship in howling gales...' but in the mess he evinced a boyish half-envious admiration for the men who flew Buccaneers and Phantoms. 'If you're living dangerously,' he said, 'it tends to make you appreciate your life that much more and to really want to live it to its fullest.'

By the very nature of helicopters, the risks permitted him reached back to the vulnerability of the warrior princes of the Middle Ages. Prince Charles has had to make several forced landings, once with computer trouble, another time when his engine started to fail, and again when a fragment of engine cover broke loose and fell into the engine. On each occasion his machine was shadowed by another helicopter with fire-fighting equipment and the Ministry of Defence made no more of the incidents than to mention 'a precautionary landing'. But the child who had needed to be entertained now, in manhood, revelled in the versatility and ever-changing experiences of helicopter flying. 'I hope and pray there'll be a chance for me to continue,' he told his Red Dragons. Prince Charles was booked, however, to take a course at the Royal Naval College, Greenwich, in the New Year of 1975, and he was also aware of a looming family landmark ahead.

In April he would reach precisely the age that his father had been when he married. 'Well,' he said, 'when you get to my extraordinary stage of decrepitude one begins to think about things like that.'

11   Chevening

I

When a young man's fancy lightly turns to thoughts of love, his reveries usually turn to the housing question only as he becomes more serious. An irrevocable break was made with his Edwardian predecessors when the Prince of Wales was ten years old and the Queen made over Marlborough House as a Commonwealth centre in London. Marlborough House, the fourth mansion or palace down the Mall from Buckingham Palace, had been earmarked for the use of either a Prince of Wales or a dowager Queen for nearly a century and, after its relinquishment to the new and colourful destiny of the Commonwealth, there remained the future prospect of York House, within the Tudor brick complex of St James' Palace. This had formerly been the bachelor home of that more recent Prince of Wales, the Duke of Windsor, but as his own coming-of-age drew near Charles had intimated that he had no thought of living there.

His decision freed useful extra space for such royal ramifications as the Chancery of the Orders of Knighthood, the Garden Party office, the needs of the Marshal of the Diplomatic Corps and offices for the advisers on the Queen's works of art, among others, and in addition a modest residential suite was devised for the London needs of the Duke and Duchess of Kent and their family. Obviously, the Queen agreed with her son that Buckingham Palace had room for both her London executive needs and his during the foreseeable future. Wood Farm meanwhile served him when required as an adequate country home instead of Sandringham House. The possibility was considered of creating a penthouse suite for the Prince amid the cavernous attics of

Hampton Court, or else perhaps one day establishing a separate domestic establishment at Kensington Palace. But into these dream homes there intruded the visions of an old gentleman who firmly believed that his country house in Kent could afford a perfect home for Prince Charles or any other member of the royal family.

Lord Stanhope, who died aged eighty-six in 1967, while Charles was preparing for his first term at Cambridge, had no children of his own and was indeed the last of a family line eminent in national life since the eighteenth century.

The seventh and last of an earldom dating from 1718, Lord Stanhope was also the thirteenth and last Earl of Chesterfield. The fourth Earl of Chesterfield, the statesman memorable for his letters of counsel to his natural son, had been the first Earl Stanhope's close kinsman. The last Lord Stanhope was Winston Churchill's immediate pre-war predecessor as First Lord of the Admiralty and Lord President of the Council during Neville Chamberlain's administration, a diligent figure through half a century of politics and public service. Yet his lack of a son was a deep misfortune, and in his declining and widowed years the future of Chevening, the family home through three centuries, weighed upon him as a sad and ever-present problem.

'Chevening – to rhyme with evening,' I was told by a friendly villager when I first went there some years ago and lost my way in the Kentish lanes. Lord Stanhope planned at first to offer the house to the nation, and he mentions in a notebook of 1943 that he went to see Winston Churchill at No. 10 'and we began to talk of my offer of Chevening as a residence for a Cabinet Minister ...' Built to a plan of Inigo Jones on earlier Tudor foundations, the house was older than the family. Plain and four-square, it had stood for nearly a century before the first Earl Stanhope purchased it the year before gaining his title and embarked upon the improvements that distinguish it today.

The seventh Earl at last saw his hopes firmly established in 1959 when the Chevening Estate Act came to the statute-book

153

and gave the force of law to a trust deed by which he made the
house to the nation as a furnished and endowed country residence,
with a carefully defined priority of occupancy beyond his own
lifetime. Under its terms it was first to be offered to the Queen
Mother, who had once stayed there with her husband, and any
lineal descendant of King George VI or their married partners,
then the Prime Minister and Cabinet Ministers, and finally the
Canadian High Commissioner in London, the United States
Ambassador or the National Trust. The Premier at that time,
Mr Harold Macmillan, wrote to Lord Stanhope appreciatively:
'Your long service to the State is crowned with a gift which will
allow the rare beauty of Chevening and its wonderful atmosphere
of peace and serenity to serve the same high purpose which you
and your forebears have always cherished.' The donor's endow-
ment of £250,000 was assured, but under his will the full sum
was found to exceed a million pounds.

The last of the line had in fact sold estates in Devon and
Derbyshire to focus his wealth on his old family home, although
ironically Chevening was never more in danger than through its
years of transition. During the war a bomb struck the building
and fortunately failed to explode, but the impact caused spreading
cracks in the brickwork and tore away part of the creamy tile
facing. When the Queen and Prince Charles first went over the
house together in the late autumn of 1969, two walls were shored
up with timbers and it can hardly be said that the visitors were
charmed at first sight. A gale was raging across the park, stripping
the trees, and every sash window in the house shook and rattled.
Shattered tiles lay about the courtyard like autumn leaves and
the place had an air of desertion. Inside the mansion, dust-sheets
had been hurriedly removed, and shutters opened to the light of
day, and there was the melancholy off-putting atmosphere of a
house overfull of old-fashioned furniture and obsolescent fittings
of every kind. 'Nothing touched,' as Charles said, 'since 1900.'
The family portraits peered through fogs of dark varnish and a

battery of ancient sporting guns hung gloomily rusting line upon line in the entrance hall.

At nineteen, Prince Charles was more interested in seeing the world than inspecting another stately museum, and the Queen was non-committal. First impressions that dark and wintry day were misleading, although an architect's report presently confirmed the advisability of looking the gift-horse firmly in the mouth. In undertaking a survey for the trustees, Mr Donald Insall found the brickwork at two corners of the main block in an acutely dangerous state, while the roof was sagging under the weight of the extra attics, chimneys and guttering added in Victorian times. A nineteenth-century innovator had faced the house with tiles carried by nine-inch nails which, driven into the brickwork, had seriously corroded, and this in turn hastened the process of decay. Altogether it presented an intimidating picture, and it was realised that the task of reconditioning to bring the house to modern standards might occupy two or three years.

'Prince Charles will definitely not be living there,' said one of the Queen's secretaries in January, 1973, and within a few months Lord Hailsham, Lord Chancellor in Mr Heath's Cabinet, moved in with his wife as the first official occupants, taking up residence in four rooms of a newly furbished staff wing while work on the main house remained unfinished. Their tenure was brief. Under the terms of the trust deed, the political occupants were required to vacate on losing office and in the following February the new Labour government came to power. Once again the Queen Mother declined the house as the first on the rota of occupants. Then at Easter Prince Charles came to Chevening again, and was enchanted.

What made him change his mind?

II

Home was the sailor, home from circling the world on the frigate

Jupiter, home to England in April. He had seen Chevening
gloomy and deserted in wintry storm, and now he saw it again
in the freshness of Spring, lawns green and mown, the trees
awakening, the waterfowl cutting their patterns on a lake, once
dank and dismal, now clear and dancing. He had seen an ageing
and dilapidated country house with too many dreary attic windows
and too many chimneys – he could have counted thirty. And
suddenly everything was fresh as paint, incredibly serene, new-
born, beautiful in every way. To say that Charles was astonished
may argue a failure of imagination, but it was so.

He saw it also through more travelled eyes, and in a decisive
contemporary context when visiting it with his father one morning by helicopter. Chevening lies only twenty-two miles south-
east from the heart of London, a mile closer to Buckingham
Palace than Windsor Castle itself and twelve minutes from the
Palace lawns by chopper across the broad riband of the Thames.
One swirls briefly above the dark roofs and busy thoroughfares
of Brixton towards the sight-lines of the green playing grounds
of Dulwich School and the television mast of the bygone Crystal
Palace and, beyond outer suburbs surprisingly verdant with
gardens and open space, the chopper crests the ridge of the
North Downs – those hills that overseas visitors consider named
with English absurdity, south of London and full of 'ups'.
Swiftly the scene changes to the region of apple orchards and
farmland that spells the difference between Surrey and Kent,
and the shifting carpet below is patterned with beechwoods and
pasture. Clearly seen from the air is the old medieval way
trodden by Chaucer's Canterbury pilgrims which crosses Chevening park to left and right. And unexpectedly, in this private
green realm, there is the classic eighteenth-century façade of the
house, seven windows wide and three floors high, dressed with
a Palladian relief of white columns against russet brickwork.

The original ordered proportions of the house have been re-
gained by replacing the top-heavy Victorian attics with a hipped
blue-grey roof enlivened by five neat and pleasant dormers. The

windows have been reglazed throughout with the delicate sash-work depicted in the early architectural pictures; and the brick-work, long hidden beneath 'mathematical' tiling, now freshly cleaned and pointed, has an attractive, elegant air. On either side, curving colonnades link the central château with its two graceful pavilions, the eastern one perhaps for domestic staff, the western an obvious haven for the secretarial staff and Household of a Prince and Princess of Wales.

The Prince has acquired an eye for such effects and is struck by a dramatic architectural coincidence. Few houses are to be found balanced in partnership with two such pavilions. In ground area, Chevening is not large; there are only six rooms on the ground floor, and there again, in elevation, it resembles the old drawings of the original Buckingham House, even to the two mansard-roofed pavilions that flank either side. Looking around the entrance hall, shortly before his nomination as tenant, Charles admired the effect of the pale oak panelling, cleaned of the grime of two centuries, and the extraordinary 'hanging stair-case', which is indeed one of the wonders of the house. Designed by Nicholas Dubois, a military engineer, it twists upwards to the second floor, like a swirling pack of cards, to all appearances supported only on its own steps, which are of solid Spanish oak, two metres wide. Beyond the square entrance hall in turn lies the arcaded 'saloon', a graceful setting of family portraits within the recessed pine arcades, a delightful party room overlooking the lake.

Living on the job, Charles is accustomed to being neighboured by a range of rarely used yet occasionally useful state apartments and, on the first floor, Chevening possesses a magnificent draw-ing-room running north to south the full length of the house. The ceiling of intricate Italian plasterwork is one of the most delicately beautiful in Britain, its glories masked until recently by greying layers of white paint until sample scrapes revealed the true pastel colourings. The marble chimney-piece is from the same workshop that equipped Versailles, and a mantelpiece

elsewhere resembles one used by Vanbrugh at Blenheim. When
Prince Charles first viewed this apartment with the Queen, the
three sumptuous chandeliers of Waterford crystal and the rich
wall sconces were part bagged up, and the floor space was cluttered by a miscellany of antique furnishings. But he next saw
the room with all its vistas cleared, and the faded wallpapers
renewed with perfect fidelity – it made all the difference.

In the adjoining Tapestry Room are wall-hangings, depicting
a theme of dancers and peacocks, that were a gift to the Stan-
hopes from Frederick I of Prussia. Some of the tapestries bear
the woven signatures of the Berlin workshop established when
the Huguenot persecutions drove the Beauvais weavers from
France. Nearby is a guest 'state bedroom' boasting the Hepplewhite four-poster bed in which the younger William Pitt often
slept after riding over to Chevening to visit his nieces. In another
bedroom on this floor the restorers, impeccably guided by Mr
John Fowler, have revived a rare Chinese wallpaper piece by
piece after cleaning and repair. Yet here the chief focus is a
carved and splendid Elizabethan four-poster bed, oak to its topmost covering, a bed surely contrived to lap its sleeper in dreams
of English tradition.

And this also reveals the appeal of the new Chevening to
Prince Charles. In a memorandum of 1965 Lord Stanhope had
specially mentioned the 'advantage particularly for the heir to
the throne to have a residence near London, even Buckingham
Palace is being overlooked from all sides, and no longer has
much privacy.' The Palace had gained a unique place as the
formal headquarters of the Crown. But in Chevening the heir to
the throne saw a country house where he could visualise enter-
taining European and Commonwealth heads of government in
his own way, where world leaders of every clime would be able
to meet in small groups while enjoying his hospitality, forging
new friendships while beneath his roof. It would be entertainment without political or government strings, informal and
eventually in a family atmosphere, like the Commonwealth itself.

Once this aspect of Chevening had won the Prince's imagination, the more persuasive it appeared.

This new idea was the essence. In America, on meeting some ladies who called themselves 'Daughters of the British Empire', as members of an association of that name, he had pressed tender nerves by asking what their British Empire was all about. 'It would make you more relevant,' he said, 'if you called yourselves "Daughters of the British Commonwealth". And when I come back next, I hope you'll be calling yourselves "Daughters of THE Commonwealth".'

III

At Chevening, again, Prince Charles would be living over the shop and, above the entertainment rooms, at the topmost flight of the celebrated staircase was an inviting second-floor suite of private apartments which he felt would be much to his taste. 'Quite a penthouse,' an American friend had said, gazing over the view of lawns and lake and treetops. On his earlier exploration the Prince had paid only casual attention to what had seemed a labyrinth of passages leading only to a warren of bedrooms. This living space was indeed sufficiently muddled to give rise to the legendary view of Chevening as a 115-room white elephant which, he had to confess, now slightly ruffled him. 'If I'd bought a poky little house of my own, I think I would have come in for criticism,' he glumly told Kenneth Harris. 'If I'd brought a big house out of my own pocket... more criticism.'

It had seemed sensible, after all, to accept his nomination to Chevening as the owner had wished. Led by the agent, Mr Burton, four of the trustees toured the house one day, meticulously counting every room, from the vaulted cellars to the attic cupboards and boxrooms, from the downstairs cloakrooms to the pavilion wings. The total was eighty-three: comprising on the ground floor the definitive three reception rooms, with a small staff sitting-room and a kitchen, on the first floor the drawing-room, the Tapestry Room, the two large bedrooms already mentioned and two others with bath and dressing-rooms. After replanning, the second floor yielded six bedrooms, four bathrooms, two dressing-rooms and a kitchenette. But Prince Charles could readily visualise the architect's sketch plan reducing this to pleasantly modern living-rooms, a study and a private bedroom suite, and any other accommodation needed.

Though still in the planning stage at this time of writing, incomplete and with little more changed than the lining paper, the atmosphere of this private milieu can be judged by the Prince's private 'pad' at the Palace, decorated under the aegis of his Mountbatten cousin-in-law, David Hicks, with small background pieces of antique furniture, some recognisable from old Osborne inventories, with comfortable chesterfields, table lamps and other accents of modern trend. In a sitting-room, which Charles prefers for business interviews, the visitor recollects tan leather armchairs, a deep yellow sofa, Eskimo soapstone carvings, and glossy books that lie about as well as cramming the shelves. In his habitual, more personal living-room are cosier deep-slung loose-covered armchairs and small open Georgian bookcases, a Gordon Russell coffee-table, and among the paintings a sparse Sidney Nolan landscape, an unexpected Venetian study by the Swansea artist Howard Roberts, and other Welsh landscapes. Homely Maltese pottery stands casually alongside Louis Osman's gold sphere of the moon, one of the five which the designer specially set aside for Charles, Mrs Rose Kennedy and the first three moonmen, Armstrong, Aldrin and Collins.

Like his father, Charles seldom visits a modern art exhibition without asking to have this or that sent to the Palace for consideration, purchases that often form Christmas or anniversary gifts to his friends. There's no arts patronage more practical than hard cash encouragement. Among modern designers, Prince Charles buys from contemporary goldsmiths and silversmiths such as Gerald Benny, Michael Drover, Keith Redfern and

Associates, Hans Gehrig of Canada, Ernest Blyth and others. In giving liquor flasks to naval friends, the choice fell on flasks by the Derbyshire silversmith, Brian Asquith, and the Prince deliberately seeks out newcomers in design from time to time.

IV

It was also a paramount consideration with Charles that Chevening was in strategic neighbourly reach of many of his closest personal friends, among them his Brabourne cousins; the Knatchbulls at Mersham; the Astors at Hever; the younger Cazalets near Shipbourne; the Nevills at Eridge and Uckfield, and the Sidneys at Penthurst. Having visited the house one day with a friend, Prince Charles then paid another visit at the weekend, when there were no workmen about, with a group of five or six young people, as if anxious to view Chevening afresh through the eyes of his contemporaries. They explored from the deep basement upwards, laughing at cellar doorways that had obviously once admitted portentously large barrels, and the old house must have warmed to their gaiety. They opened a picnic hamper in the rose garden and, glancing down at them, an estate veteran thought how pleasant it was to hear young voices about the place.

They strolled through the avenues of ancient yew and linden south of the lake and no doubt inspected what locals irreverently call 'the dogs' cemetery', the ancient Roman tombstones which the first Earl Stanhope brought home from the Spanish wars, given to him by the citizens of Tarrragona as a token of gratitude. They would have seen the outsize Chatham Vase, the largest garden ornament in Kent, commissioned as a family memorial in 1781; indeed, where else is there a counterpart except perhaps the fifteen-foot marble Waterloo Vase in the garden of Buckingham Palace? An extraordinary Eden to survive on the administrative verge of the county of London, the

Chevening estate extends over three thousand five hundred acres, which incorporate magnificent beechwoods and parkland, farms and hamlets, and defies casual reconnaissance.

The fourth Earl Stanhope, who died in 1855, solemnly enjoined in a codicil to his will that 'the sight and arrangement of the said gardens' should be preserved unaltered to future ages, a wish difficult of fulfilment. Palm trees flourish north-east of the house, so sheltered is the situation, but they are past their prime. The parterre-style flower beds have an out-moded air, as unrefreshing and unhelpful as the enormous collection of old gardening books, valuable but useless, that encumber the library shelves.

A codicil is an afterthought made lawful, though the dead hand is open to wider interpretation, and to one of his friends Prince Charles has listened with intent attention, regarding himself as an ignoramus against her own knowledge of plants and flowers and garden lay-out. 'When you have something which is *almost* your own you want to make a transformation,' he has confided. 'I'm really rather excited at the prospect of trying to lay out something, planting things, and making rides in the woods.'

The more he becomes acquainted with Chevening and its history, the more such sidelight topics vivaciously recur in table talk. On succeeding to the title in 1786, the third Earl, for example, struck a Stanhope Medal inscribed 'Stanhope the friend of Trial by Jury, Liberty of the Press, Parliamentary Reform, Annual Parliaments, Habeas Corpus, etc.' A notable figure for conversation, he so favoured the aims of the French Revolution that he took down the coronets from the Chevening gates and was pleased to be known as 'Citizen Stanhope'. Of an inventive turn of mind, he devised not only a new printing press and an improved calculating machine, but also a system of fireproofing, which he so conclusively demonstrated in a wooden house in the grounds that, while an intense fire melted the glass window panes of the lower room, 'the Lord Mayor of London and many other persons enjoyed the luxury of ice-cream in the flame-protected room above.'

While steamboats were still an impractical idea, the lively third Earl staged a steam voyage with a working model on the Chevening lake, and the first steam paddleboat built to his principles under Admiralty auspices sailed on the Thames in 1790, eleven years before the Scottish claim of steam navigation on the Clyde. Equally early as a pioneer of woman's lib, his eldest daughter, Lady Hester Stanhope, who was born at Chevening, gained a firm hold in the popular imagination when she ran away to Constantinople with a lover. Deserted after this passionate affair, not to mention her other amours, she remained in Turkey, wearing Turkish male attire and led a life of eccentric travel in the Middle East until her innumerable adventures passed into folklore.

Her cousin, the fourth Earl, was similarly an endearing character, with so firm a belief in aviation – and this in the first decade of Queen Victoria's reign – that he invested money in an 'Aerial Courier Company... of inestimable advantage for the conveyance of despatches'. Another of his losers was Kaspar Hauser, the mysterious youth who was found wandering in Nuremburg one day in 1828 with a bewildered air, and became the topic of all Europe under the popular impression that he might be the despoiled and defrauded heir to a fortune. The enigma was as strange and debatable as that of the supposed Czarist survivor, Princess Anastasia, in the twentieth century, and the fourth Earl virtually adopted him until after prolonged enquiry, he became more sceptical of the growing discrepancies in his story. One of the few relics of the Kaspar Hauser affair today is the curious picture of the 'child of Europe' in the print gallery at Chevening, a corridor collection of portraits of notable guests and others in the mansion's long history.

In the library, the thousands of rare books have enjoyed refurbishment under the skilled care of volunteer members of the National Association of Decorative and Fine Arts Societies, who devoted three years to their labour of love. And among the books borrowed at an early stage by the new occupant was an illustrated volume, *Furniture of Chevening*, which has evidently led to deep whirlpools of discussion.

All the Stanhope furnishing goes with the house, from tapestries to table silver, gilded early Georgian looking-glasses and overmantels to complete sets of furniture by Chippendale, Hepplewhite and other pieces of the great period of English furnishing. A particular pride is the suite comprising a mahogany-legged sofa and ten matching armchairs covered with Beauvais tapestry of about the year 1751, three years before Chippendale published his 'Director' ... but who can dare to sit upon such pieces?

There are lacquer chests and cabinets, commodes and console tables, each worth a king's ransom, and all now restored and shining with subtle care. There are gilded settees, arrays of Chinese porcelain, and more sober heirlooms of the time of William and Mary. Only at Chevening, one feels, could three pieces of early Georgian silver by Paul de Lamerie be dismissed in an expert inventory as 'charming but unimportant'.

There are, perhaps, a few too many family portraits, Ramsays and Knellers, for some tastes, but they include three Gainsboroughs. The portrait of the Earl of Chesterfield in its place of honour above the drawing-room chimney-piece belongs to the best years when the artist was winning celebrity in Bath. Elsewhere at Chevening is reputedly the last portrait that Gainsborough ever painted, inevitably another Stanhope, a young man in Parliamentary robes who amusingly resembles Prince Charles himself. All these treasures set new responsibilities and new riddles for the occupant. Old photographs in the Trust files show the pieces in their time-honoured places as they were once arranged in the various rooms, but the rows of mahogany and rosewood, interrupted only by gigantic sergeant-major vases, could not long be endured. This is not to be a stately home displayed for the hordes, nor yet to be set out with any suggestion of a museum. In their ultimate rearrangement, the Charles II chairs and the collection of swords, the paintings and curios, even the display cabinet with a treasured lock of hair from William Pitt and a passport signed by Oliver Cromwell, must all still grace the house, though with a hint of its new master.

On his personal bookshelves Charles treasures an illustrated book showing Clarence House as furnished and freshly decorated in his mother's day. The pictures embellish his memories of his own early childhood and, when his home in Kent is again settled and lived in, Charles is inclined to publish a similar volume to enable everyone to enjoy through text and camera the spirit of the recreated Chevening of his own. But there are others to be consulted in the new era and as he awaited the key, a handsome eighteenth-century specimen to fit a brass lock of $14\frac{1}{2}$ inches by $7\frac{1}{2}$ inches, there also remained the highly romantic enigma of his partner in the enterprise.

12 A Princess for Wales

I

During the Chevening prelude, throughout all the activity about the estate in the summer of 1975, the local people had good cause to wonder whether the future châtelaine could not be espied among the innumerable visitors to the mansion. Was there no prospective lady of the house to consult in all the problems of furnishing and landscaping, no sign of feminine choice in all the questions that the inscrutable John Fowler and his associates settled stage by stage? When Prince Charles' future tenancy of Chevening was first announced, the press stood to as if at a flashing alert, and yet unexpectedly showed sympathy and forebearance in not raising false alarms. Invited to take part in a matter of insurance on a royal wedding, a London bookmaker demurred at laying odds after considering the past statistics. Prince Charles was twenty-seven on November 14th, 1975, older by seven months than his father had been on entering marriage. His grandfather, King George VI, had married aged twenty-seven and four months; his great-grandfather, George V, at twenty-eight and one week. In the present generation, the Duke of Gloucester had married at twenty-seven, and the Duke of Kent at twenty-five.

While the Prince hurtled about the world, from the high Himalayas to independence celebrations in Papua, the possibility of his marriage had become one of the most frequent questions put to the Press Secretariat at Buckingham Palace. With an air of appealing confidentiality, the Palace maintained that there were no girls in his life. No girls, it was said, and in evidence Charles was very obviously 'extremely busy' with his helicopters, his Welsh conservancy and overseas travel. Perhaps it could not be helped if foreign conclusions were drawn of bachelor celibacy or if the enquirer were left reflecting on the Duke of Windsor's arid devotions to two or three ladies before he met Mrs Simpson at the age of thirty-six.

Early in 1975 Charles flew off with the Duke and Duchess of Gloucester to attend the coronation of the year, the crowning of twenty-eight year-old King Birendra of Nepal in the feverishly scrubbed and flower-decked city of Katmandu. Socially and royally, this proved a great lark, all but on the roof of the world. The Crown Prince of Japan arrived with three truckloads of luggage and fifteen cases of Fuji mineral water, and a brace of Eton housemasters celebrated on soft drinks with a quartet of Harvard tutors. It was a glorious and festive occasion: the Duchess of Gloucester danced with President Marcos of the Philippines, while the Prince jived with the beautiful Madame Marcos, and Earl Mountbatten appeared 'a delightfully wicked elderly gent' to a sophisticated new generation of eastern princesses. After being anointed with mud, the old Etonian King Birendra was ritually cleansed with yoghourt and honey and his crowning occurred on the propitious day and at the unfeasible hour of eight thirty-seven a.m., appointed by court astrologers. Was it also an auspicious sign, equal to any watched by Birendra's astrologers, that early in the year Prince Charles had an appointment with the Archbishop of Canterbury?

The Prince had announced this so solemnly that some swallowed the bait, but the jester was at work. In fact, he was attending the enthronement of the new Archbishop, Dr Coggan, in Canterbury Cathedral, a ceremony princes have shunned for centuries. The topic lightly arose that Canterbury might be a more convenient venue for a wedding than Westminster Abbey. Merely as a conversational game, Charles enjoys matching old precedents against new possibilities.

Discovering that his traditional place in the Lords was on the steps of the throne, he casually strolled into the House one afternoon and sat on the carpeted steps to hear a defence debate. On making his second speech to the Lords a few weeks later, he took a customary place on the cross-benches. Like his father, he takes pains with his speeches, drafting and revising, memorising and often seeming to speak extempore, though a copy lies to hand. The Willie Hamiltons who wonder how the Prince passes his time when not playing polo, may overlook the hours with tape and typewriter. The summer debate on community service supplied a theme on which he felt he could contribute useful and not inexpert views. 'Voluntary service is good for the soul, as beneficial to the volunteer as to the recipient, and an essential element in any society calling itself civilised . . .' He put the nub in the opening sentence and commended the organisations which were already involving the young in imaginative and adventurous new forms of useful endeavour. He had already, he said, been pursuing an idea to help the anti-social and more alienated sections of young people. He failed to mention that he had personally met much of the expense of setting up pilot schemes to that end.

A youth placed on probation after violently assaulting a schoolmaster found himself put in touch with a teenage group who were making themselves dinghies for sea-fishing expeditions. It took him time to learn that the idea was sponsored by Charles as part of the so-called Dreadnought scheme, launched under the cumbersome name of the Prince of Wales Scheme for Disadvantaged Young People. In the Solent, a counterpart scheme involves young locals in the excitement of inshore rescue work. In Glamorgan the Prince has signed the cheques for planting, oak, ash and beech on the green hillsides instead of the deadening spruce, and the tree-planting volunteers come up from the towns in truckloads. The Prince is convinced that, in a modest way, such ideas offer a practical antidote to the boredom of hanging about street corners and bus shelters.

The Queen Mother has long kept a chiding notice on her desk which says 'Do It Now'. Prince Charles might match the memo with 'Try it now', with his constant zeal for something new to attempt. No previous heir to the throne had ever ventured to the Commons side of Parliament, but an invitation to lunch with the members of the House of Commons Press Gallery was accordingly accepted with alacrity, an opportunity for words of amusing candour. Skating on thin ice, the Prince demonstrated his awareness of every rippling current in the ceaseless surmise that surrounds his unmarried status; 'unaccustomed as I am to unveiling busts', as he once put it, on tugging the drapes from a bronze of his father. Exposing himself was different, he told the journalists; the scrutiny of his life 'was predictably to be expected. There had been that crowd of ten thousand, gathered to see a certain young lady at Sandringham. I almost felt I had better espouse myself at once. As you can see, I thought better of it...' All the same, he could 'move around a little', although 'it becomes more difficult to potter gently through the streets.'

This was the week of the Moorgate Underground disaster and, on the spur of the moment after the Gallery session, Charles characteristically called at St Bartholomew's hospital to comfort and encourage as many as he could among the injured, and sympathise with the harried medical staff. Similarly, when men of the Welsh Guards were terribly maimed in a pub bombing, their royal Colonel-in-Chief found it as essential to visit them in hospital as if they had been his closest friends. This is traditional royal duty, yet Charles felt genuinely thankful that he could have some share in the therapy.

The ruled columns of Prince Charles' engagement book and his EA (Engagement Accepted) cards give insufficient clues to a widening daily round intermixed with Service schedules and with business flowing into pleasure. The Prince was formally called to the Bar and made an honorary bencher of Gray's Inn, a customary ceremony for which the central figure refrained from sagging jokes about propping up the Establishment. On becoming Patron of the Royal Opera, he showed his happy view

of the distinction by arranging a party of five friends to see
Traviata from the royal box, taking pride in staging a dinner
party in the private dining-room between the acts and footing
the bill later, a classic tincture of Edward VII's precedents. In
Edwardian days opportunities of princely service moved along
well-defined and conventional channels. Prince Charles hewed
a new line when the Royal Anthropological Institute enquired
if he might like to be involved in a television series in their
field. And why not?

It stemmed, of course, from Prince Philip's proved willingness
to extend any major patronage by television and to make persuasive appearances for causes as varied as wild life conservation
and the salvage of stately homes. At an R.A.I. dinner, Prince
Charles had a eloquently spoken of the need to popularising anthropology as a source of knowledge of the motivations of man-
kind. The sequel was, of course, a race of television companies to
secure him for their cameras, and his agreement to take part in a
series to feature himself and others giving a personal view of
'the values of Man', much as Kenneth Clark had done in his
Civilisation. Location work with a film unit, it was explained,
might depend on naval duties and yet might well be linked with
them.

II

Brought up on Van Dyck, remembering from childhood seeing
his mother wearing State robes or evening dress at the oddest
times of day while sitting for her portrait, Prince Charles could
regard royal portraiture as one of the more tedious chores of his
profession. Painters and sculptors find it difficult to pin him
down to appointments for sittings. When they have him at last,
in flying kit, military uniform, velvet robes, they find him an
'almost compulsive talker' ... 'talkative ... conversationally inclined', a sitter who prefers to get better acquainted with the
artist rather than sharpen the visual images of royal mythology

or submit too often to the probing scrutiny of the artistic eye. Yet there remains an experiment in face-to-face confrontation, another bargain with the media tested initially when Prince Philip was one of the first royals to yield to the importunities of editors for on-the-record interviews. Prince Charles triumphantly established before his investiture that if he could successfully undergo prolonged interrogation by television commentators he was ready for all comers ... and very probably all questions.

In the early years of her reign, when the Queen gave official sittings to as many as six different artists in a year, from Annigoni to Seago, no authors or journalists were accorded a parallel privilege. Even Prince Philip seemed immune from the reporter's sound-tape. 'If we do it for one, we must do it for all,' said Richard Colville, the then Palace press secretary, which was undeniably nonsense, but it was not until 1962 that Prince Philip received Kenneth Harris of *The Observer* without feeling obliged to welcome writers from every newspaper. Two years passed before Peter Lewis of the *Daily Mail* won a similar recognition. Ten years later, no time at all to the recording angel, Charles welcomed the gifted Ann Leslie of the *Mail* for two linked interviews, though putting it to her that he felt he could be more frank and helpful if not directly quoted. Two months later, this reservation was thrown to the winds for a long question-and-answer conversation with Kenneth Harris, and early in 1975 the London *Evening Standard* announced the scoop of its young news editor, Stuart Kuttner, with uninhibited question sessions against backgrounds royal and various as Buckingham Palace and Yeovilton airfield.

The ghost of Dr Johnson, who had once found himself in unexpected and leisurely conversation with George III in the library of Buckingham House, must have looked down approvingly on such compelling topics as the lone and separate quality of the Prince of Wales' position and his deliberate techniques of leadership, his pleasures and discomforts in naval duty and the Prince's express admiration of George III, 'his incredible capacity for hard work and his conscientious devotion to duty'.

Whole eras have been telescoped since Harold Nicolson undertook to write the official biography of King George V – this in the year Prince Charles was born, as it happened – and was testily reminded by the Palace that he would be 'writing a book about a very ancient national institution and need not descend to personalities.' Such hoodoos have acquired an unacceptable shabbiness, strongly conflicting with the candour of Prince Charles' opinion that honesty is best. Kenneth Harris enquired to what extent, as a serving officer, Prince Charles was conscious of being a monarch-to-be. 'I'm much more conscious,' said Charles, 'of being a Prince of Wales-as-is.' The question of being 'different' was raised, and Charles logically asked how he could know or tell *how much* different he was. One could only deduce things about other people. 'I've had the background I've had and not many other people have had that.' The fallacies of not being able to mix, of not gaining friends outside a limited circle, raised their dragon-like heads and were extinguished. None of us can mix with everyone. For every individual, acquaintance or friendship are matters of circumstance.

Prince Charles found that he enjoyed searching his conscience, so to speak, at first sight of a written list of questions, girding himself for the impromptu element to follow. Looking back on the educational pattern that had helped shape his personality, would he prescribe the same for his son? Did he watch television much? The replies, though often predictable, helped to clarify his public image, even to some degree to himself. Gordonstoun and the Services had indeed given strength, discipline and deeper responsibility. Watching television depended, like so much else, on the time factor, although he adored the Goodies, 'exactly my sense of humour'.

The preliminary typed questions were for preparation, not for side-stepping, and in any event the Prince was apt to suggest themes of his own. 'Is there really a large body of opinion that I should give up polo? Even if you feel it does no harm, people's susceptibilities count.' The 'philistine image' of the royal family could be misleading. 'If newspapers happen to show me playing polo and never show me going to the opera, the image would be one of a polo-player...' In the congenial warmth of the interview, Kenneth Harris touched on the deeper problem that if the monarch lives long and remains on the Throne, is the heir-apparent not 'kept out'? 'Doesn't it depend,' Charles countered, 'on what I make of things? Precisely because I am *not* the Sovereign and therefore not so bound by the Constitution, there's a wider range of possibilities of contributing.'

In dispelling steamy illusions, in the exercise of making his real personality better known, the 'conversations' have been shown to serve their purpose... if used sparingly. Too much column space and one becomes a monumental bore. Too little candour and at once the legends multiply. Among the interviews during 1974 and 1975 questioners of every calibre realised that Charles was always primed and viligant, no matter how delicate the question or diffident the approach. Ann Leslie discovered 'an inner remoteness, a secret still-centre...' Stuart Kuttner considered that the Prince 'nurtured an unswerving protective-ness about his private life'... 'Take marriage, for instance,' said Kenneth Harris tentatively, and a steely expert wariness immediately gleamed within that easy, engaging frankness, giving little away.

Prince Charles would talk freely on the happy, close-knit family life he had always enjoyed. 'I'm happier at home, with the family, than anywhere else,' he once said. Marriage, he hoped, would merely lift that kind of happiness into another dimension with a partner whose interests one understood and could share. From the woman's point of view, said Charles, 'she not only marries a man; she marries into a way of life, into a job, a life in which she's got a contribution to make. She's got to have some knowledge of it, some sense of it, or she wouldn't have a clue about whether she's going to like it...' Both to Harris and Kuttner, the Prince spoke of 'deciding on whom one wants to live with for fifty years ... one of the biggest and most responsible steps to be taken in one's life.' And to Kuttner he emphasised, 'My marriage has to be for ever.' Which was a better way of expressing it, less off-putting for the girl, than the naïve and clumsy phrasing he had used at twenty, 'When you marry, in my position, you are going to marry somebody who perhaps one day is going to be Queen. You've got to choose somebody very carefully, I think, who could fulfil this particular role.'

Heading towards his twenty-seven birthday, he had sufficient insight to recognise when his illusions were in transition. Marriage is not necessarily a romantic idea about 'falling madly in love and having a love affair for the rest of your married life.' Compatibility has to come into it, 'shared interests and ideas in common and also a great deal of affection'. It sounded very much as if someone had seriously remonstrated that the relationship stretched beyond glamorous romance and that love was 'basically a very strong affection'. He used these very words, and Stuart Kuttner felt empowered to ask, 'Have you a particular girl in mind?'

'Well, that would be letting too much out of the bag, wouldn't it,' Prince Charles mysteriously responded. 'Obviously, there must be someone, somewhere, for me.' Transposed into another key, it sounded indeed as if there were someone, though as yet he was not telling where ...

III

In the Household dining-room at Buckingham Palace, that clubable dining-hall of the secretarial upper echelons, the atmosphere is more relaxed when the Queen is away. It can be pleasantly gossipy as a village, yet each man and women hugs a private perquisite of secrets, scraps of personal royal knowledge never bandied around. Early in 1975, a lieutenants' course scheduled for Prince Charles at the Royal Naval College, Greenwich, was deferred ... and the air of surmise that over-hung the dining-room was as obvious as the starchy fragrance of the table-linen. The home-based Greenwich course would have kept the Prince comfortably in touch with London social pleasures. Instead, he was taking on something much tougher, a rota of commando support training with the helicopters of 845 Naval Air Squadron, first with a preliminary assault course of the muscle-straining Tarzan-swinging kind which Charles had already sampled and termed 'most horrifying', and then service with a chopper unit aboard the carrier *Hermes*.

Meanwhile, the Prince alertly kept fit, taking six a.m. alarm calls from the Windsor switchboard, ready to go energetically riding across the Lambourn gallops at dawn with Princess Anne, seeing more of his married sister than he had for months, even to fox-hunting on a rainy February day with the Beaufort and enjoying another fog-shrouded day in her company at a meet of the Cottesmore.

Sympathetic readers will realise that wild horses, let alone hunters, cannot draw the name of any other young lady to these pages until Charles' own definition of 'strong affection' avowedly transfers to stronger emotional levels. Among the Prince's friends, one young man, as interested in social anthropology and behaviourism as the regal top-notch himself, has reminded me that Hermes, with his winged sandals and herald's staff, is one of the associative Greek gods of love. An eager swain could hardy be under a better divinity when wishing to demonstrate his courage, strength and endurance to his lady. When it was known that the tour of *Hermes* was to include not merely exercises in home waters and the mid-Atlantic, but also three months between the West Indies and Canada, the suspicion grew like a summer cloud that the voyage might represent one of those ordained separations so often inflicted on princes or princesses to test whether hearts had grown fonder. The well-tried royal tradition is that the young couple should endure an interlude apart to be all the more certain of themselves before announcing their betrothal. It happened with the Queen's family journey to South Africa, as Princess Elizabeth, before she joyfully returned home to Philip. It could be seen in Katharine Worsley's long stay in Canada before her engagement to the Duke of Kent. It motivated Princess Alexandra's journey around the world the year before she married Angus Ogilvy.

Even within a small but highly knowledgeable circle the indications moved in double harness. A demi-royal wedding at Chester Cathedral that Spring, the marriage of the Queen's camera-happy second cousin, Lord Lichfield, to Lady Leonora Grosvenor, bore happy scrutiny as the possible harbinger of events to come. The one thousand five hundred wedding guests included the Queen, the Queen Mother and Princess Margaret, King Constantine and Queen Anne-Marie of the Hellenes, Princess Beatrix of the Netherlands, Earl Mountbatten and so forth; and elderly aunts recalled that at just such a wedding, thirty years ago, that of Earl Mountbatten's daughter, Patricia, to Lord Brabourne at Romsey Abbey, Elizabeth and Philip had first been seen together in public. The hopeful who noted an atmosphere of anticipation in the Gothic setting of Chester Cathedral might as well have expected to see the Prince of Wales in his coronet as Earl of Chester. He had, in fact, already expressed regrets to Lord Lichfield for his absence. This was the last weekend before his return to naval service, and he had a prior and private appointment in his own private world.

Prince Charles received special leave, indeed, to defer reporting to H.M.S. *Hermes* until two hours before sailing, and his naval helicopter swerved past the towering cranes of the Devonport docks and touched down on a flight deck cluttered with military vehicles, 'to the inch and the minute', not an easy landing. Many of his fellow pilots had trained with him at Yeovilton, and the marines of 42 Commando group were the men with whom he had tackled the rope walks and slush tunnels at Lympstone.

The following week they were all involved in assault landings with Dutch and American troops under acute conditions of mimic warfare, and the pelting rain seemed more in keeping than their anticipations of Caribbean sunshine.

During these exercises, Prince Charles received word that the wife of one of his closest friends, Tommy Sopwith, had been tragically killed in a helicopter crash in Wiltshire. Though somewhat older than Charles, they had often entertained him at Compton Manor during his Portsmouth shore-leave from H.M.S. *Minerva*, and it distressed him at being so far away at such a time. It was not until mid-April, while visiting Earl Mountbatten in the Bahamas, that he learned what had occurred. Mrs Sopwith had been a qualified helicopter pilot and was flying to Hereford with her instructor when the aircraft had dropped like a stone.

Life is trimmed with strange embroidery. On April 23rd Charles began an official visit to Canada where, on the very first day, he was due to inspect the National Aircraft Collection in Ottawa, and found himself sitting in the cockpit of one of the First World War Sopwith Snipes that will always be associated with Tommy's family.

IV

The Canadian crowds were far larger than the authorities had expected, the scenes at sports arenas, exhibition halls and concerts far more welcoming than was foreseen. The quirky *Toronto Star* wrote of 'blue-rinsed matrons nearly pushing police escorts into glass-panelled walls, women dissolving shrieking and quivering as the bachelor heir touched their hands and passed by.' At the Government House ball in Ottawa a gasping woman reporter shadowed him throughout the evening until Charles remedied this by taking her onto the dance floor where starry-eyed shock restored her to order. From these frissons the

Prince flew to Frobisher Bay to visit the North-West Territories earlier in the year than his parents had ever done, and so experienced the frontier atmosphere and polar zest before the snow and ice had thawed. One heard of his arrival at Grise Fiord, the most northerly Eskimo settlement within the Arctic Circle, closer to the North Pole than London to John o'Groat's, and next day he was out with an Eskimo guide and a husky-drawn sled mushing across the snow in search of caribou. He had a Yellowknife fixture to go down a 3,500 ft deep gold mine; another mission to a natural gas field 'replenishing my jokes'; and he dashingly drove the brightest blue and red snow-mobile ever seen to attend a local jamboree of Eskimo games.

He took a lesson in building an igloo 'in case the heating fails back home'. Far from home though never far from reporters, he looked 'dogged up' in his wolverine-trimmed blue parka: 'I hope we don't meet a polar bear, he might think I'm in season.' When the Press corps composed and chorused a song about their task of keeping up with him 'over the ice floes', Charles had a response composed and ready for his own team next night,

> *'Disgraceful, most dangerous to share the same plane*
> *Denies me the chance to scratch and complain.*
> *Oh where may I ask is the monarchy going,*
> *When Princes and Pressmen share the same Boeing?'*

Yet the *clou* of the Territories trip was the moment at the underwater research station at Resolute Bay when, partnered by Joe MacInnis, a young scientist credited with being the first man ever to swim beneath the North Pole, the Prince made a diving descent to the Arctice sea-bed through a hole in the ice already freezing over, as he wrote, rather like a *crème de menthe frappée*. The ice was six feet thick, the water temperature 28·5 degrees Fahrenheit, and the depth to the ocean floor thirty feet.

In his rubber 'variable-volume' diving suit, 'like a great orange walrus', Charles surfaced briefly to collect a lamp for photography and altogether swam around beneath the ice for thirty minutes. 'Without protective clothing a man would freeze in thirty seconds,' Dr MacInnis kindly informed him afterwards. Having concealed suitably British props in the chilly depths beforehand, the Canadian clowned for the underwater camera by donning a bowler-hat above his diving outfit and walking with an open umbrella upside down against the ice. Charles countered by reappearing to the assembled cameramen on the surface with his diving suit absurdly inflated by compressed air, looking like a burly caricature of Edward VII, so exhilarated, as one pressman said, 'that he was overtaken by a sort of euphoric daftness'.

Millions saw the resulting television and news pictures as the princely President of the British Sub-Aqua Club then took a comic bow, slowly allowing himself to deflate and shrink like a let-down balloon. In London, the Queen Mother 'laughed all day' after seeing a full set of photographs, recalling from her Glamis childhood the cautionary tale of the Michelin man who 'bounced and bounced till they strewed the courtyard with tintacks to puncture him'. And now it was Charles who bounced and bounced everywhere, his primrose path strewn with tintacks of a different order.

Within twenty-four hours, he bounced from Resolute Bay to Miami Beach, from forty-five degrees below to seventy-five above. There he visited the Variety Club Children's Hospital with cotside bonhomie and spent a weekend with Mr and Mrs Robert Greene, who had arranged to stage a dinner party for eighty to raise funds for Variety International and pay among other things for boats to take crippled children joy-riding on the Montgomeryshire Canal. *Hermes* was usefully anchored at Port Everglades, and at eight a.m. next morning Charles was aboard with his squadron to sail to New Brunswick for a month of helicopter liaison with the R.C.A.F. air base at Blissville.

V

Blissville. The name evoked smiles. Apt or otherwise, one couldn't tell. At the end of May, when Prince Charles briefly flew back to London, he had grown a beard, reminding some of the picturesque Vandyke Philip had grown in the Navy during his earliest phase of courting Elizabeth. As an impressive example of regal speed, his plane from Canada touched down at seven forty-five a.m., and at ten thirty a.m. he was at Westminster Abbey to rehearse the ancient ceremonial for his installation next day as Great Master of the Order of the Bath. If the beard was a nautical joke for family or friends, it was reduced to a military moustache to suit his Welsh Guards uniform next morning, and twenty-four hours later a clean-shaven Charles flew off to rejoin his ship in Nova Scotia.

Among England's orders of knighthood, the Bath ranks second only to the Garter; and for a day the Abbey had echoed to fanfares, the ring of spurs, the rasp of unsheathed swords. The Queen and her knights were figures of medieval pageantry rustling in silken mantles, and solemnly the deep voice of Prince Charles promised 'to honour God, to be steadfast in the Faith, to love the Queen . . . to defend maidens, widows and orphans in their rights . . .' His installation marked the 250th anniversary of an occasion when George I had actually bathed with his knights in token of purity, but the symbolism had probably never been indulged with greater understanding than by the twentieth-century Prince, fully aware as an anthropologist of the ceremonies of preparation practised among many peoples before a marriage.

But Charles was back in London in June in readiness to ride in the Trooping the Colour ceremony for the first time . . . which involved him, incidentally, in wearing the heavy traditional bearskin headgear on the hottest summer day ever recorded. On home leave, he was also concerned with Lord Brabourne in making a documentary film about the British Legion, travelling by chopper to the Legion's poppy factory at Richmond on one side of London and its 'industrial village' at Maidstone on the other. He conversed for television with Alastair Cooke, making a spirited defence of George III, and together with the anthropology television series, a film on the restoration needs of Canterbury Cathedral, a goon-comic amateur production made as a lark in the Arctic, an intro to a television programme on Welsh architecture and a documentary on his helicopter work, the Prince was involved in seven different productions.

In the promotion of Architectural Year he had agreed to inspect the buildings renovated in Windsor, a stroll that turned into a hand-shaking, back-patting walkabout, milling among thousands of people. He opened an American War of Independence exhibition, visited a volunteer battalion of the Royal Regiment of Wales in camp on the Isle of Man, and he assisted the Queen in a Palace luncheon for Nigerian military chieftains. In July he was at Holyroodhouse to welcome his friend, King Carl Gustav of Sweden, on a state visit to Britain. After fulfilling duties in Wales, he then visited the Royal Agricultural Show at Kenilworth, and solemnly enquired whether chickens were specially bred to lay long eggs for pie centres. He sat in at an Old Bailey trial and saw sentence passed on a bomb hoaxer. He appeared unexpectedly with the naval polo team at the Royal Tournament at Earls Court. He led the review of the Cumberland Fleet at Cowes and turned up at short notice at the wreck of the Tudor warship, *Mary Rose*, off Portsmouth, enthusiastically diving around the ship, the first royal to set eyes on her since Henry VIII. In Cornwall thirty thousand people watched a naval air display and the commentators failed to mention that Charles was certainly the first Duke of Cornwall to pilot a helicopter over his own lands in a mock assault. On August 2nd he choppered to Cambridge to collect his Master of Arts degree. The impatient had some sense that the Prince was filling in time, like a man treading water. The ranks of the knowledgeable were becoming confused, while even among those close to him the Prince kept his own counsel.

Were there not similar delays – and dismaying trepidations among friends – before his grandfather won Lady Elizabeth Bowes-Lyon? In his official biography of King George VI, Sir John Wheeler-Bennett mentions that, indeed, 'Lady Elizabeth entertained a very natural reluctance to abandon the unfettered liberty of a great family for the restricted freedom of member-ship of the royal circle, where every action was public property, every step must be watched, every word guarded . . .' History is always in danger of repeating itself. The right girl could indeed fall truly in love with the Prince and yet flinch from all the diffi-culties of renouncing everyday life to fulfil a destiny of high duty as Princess of Wales. And against the background of economic stress in Britain a decision or an announcement of a royal betrothal might well be deferred.

Our present chronicle may close with the seventy-fifth birth-day of that same Lady Elizabeth – the Queen Mother – when more than seventy friends and relations gathered at Buckingham Palace for her anniversary dinner party and, curiously, the most notable absentee was her eldest grandson, who had undertaken 'a private fishing trip to Iceland'. Some suspected a hoax, and half-expected him to appear as the jubilant surprise of the evening. But the Icelandic ambassador had seen him off at the airport, and the Prince had indeed gone fishing with a group of his own friends in the cascades and pools of the Hosfar river in quest of the most magnificent salmon in the world.

Truth, like human nature itself, is indeed as strange as wishful fiction. As we turn the page, Prince Charles has under-taken his first naval command in the minehunter *Bronington*. Yet events move on, the author's typescript becomes this printed book, and perhaps, reader, in viewing the passing pageant, you may already know the happy sequel.

Select Bibliography

BOOKS

Prince Charles: Monarch in the Making – Douglas Liversidge (Arthur Barker, 1975)
To Be a King – Dermot Morrah (Hutchinson, 1968)
Prince of Wales – L. G. Pine (Herbert Jenkins, 1959)
The Queen and Her Children – Lady Peacock (Hutchinson, 1961)
The Heir Apparent – Geoffrey Wakeford (Robert Hale, 1967)

BOOKS WITH A FOREWORD OR CONTRIBUTION BY PRINCE CHARLES

King George III – John Brooke (Constable, 1972)
The Living World of Animals – (Reader's Digest, 1970)
More Goon Show Scripts – Spike Milligan (Woburn Press, 1973)
Nobs and Nosh – Allen Warren (Leslie Frewin, 1974)
The Puffin Annual (No. 1) (1974)
The World Under-water Book (The Diver, 1973)
Captains and Kings – Neville Birch and Alan Bramson (Pitman, 1972)

ESSAYS AND JOURNALISM, ETC. BY PRINCE CHARLES

Timbertop or Beating Around the Bush (Gordonstoun Record, 1966)
First Impressions of Cambridge (Varsity, March 9, 1968)
Arctic Diving (Triton, Journal of British Sub-Aqua Club, Jan. 1976)

INTERVIEWS, ETC. WITH PRINCE CHARLES

Prince Charles – A radio interview with Jack de Manio, March, 1969

Prince Charles – An interview with R. Gomer Jones (*Daily Mail, Daily Express*, etc. June, 1969)

Prince Charles – A conversation with Kenneth Harris (*The Observer*, June 9 & 16, 1974)

Prince Charles – A conversation with Stuart Kuttner (*Evening Standard*, Jan. 7 & 8, 1975)

Prince Charles – An interview with Douglas Keay (*Woman's Own*, Nov. 15, 1975)

FILM AND TELEVISION MATERIAL

A Prince for Wales – produced by David Frost (Drummond Films, 1969)

Prince Charles – A television talk to Cliff Michelmore and Brian Connell (*The Listener*, July 3, 1969)

Royal Family – produced by Richard Cawston (Joint I.T.V. and B.B.C., 1969)

Pilot Royal – produced by Josephine Douglas, directed by Christopher Doll, (B.B.C., 1975)

Prince Charles and Canterbury Cathedral – produced by Tony Maylam (Worldmark Productions, 1975)

A Much Maligned Monarch – A television talk with Alastair Cooke, (A.T.V., 1976)